MW01482454

1

Mister Chuck Explains It All

Mister Chuck Explains It All

Four Seasons in Snohomish County

Chuck Sigars

For Julie Kae

CONTENTS

Winter

"The coldest winter I ever spent was a summer in San Francisco."

--Mark Twain

"Perhaps I am a bear, or some hibernating animal underneath, for the instinct to be half asleep all winter is so strong in me."

--Anne Morrow Lindbergh

"Snowmen melt ugly. They decompensate, they drip from the top down, like the Nazis in "Raiders of the Lost Ark" at the end. You want to turn your head and not think about that Frosty song."

--*Under The Weather*, page 16

Farewells

I am writing to you from the year 2007. Greetings, people of the future! Are there flying cars yet?

I'm sure you'd find 2007 primitive and ignorant. For example, we still don't know if the Patriots went 16-0, while that must seem like ancient history to you.

On the other hand, it's snowing like crazy here in this time period.

It's become a cliché that we now live in the future, that technology advances exponentially and changes our lives on a daily basis. This is true, too; even 10 years ago we would have been surprised, I think, at how routine we find cell phones, MP3 players, ubiquitous WiFi and Britney Spears.

My wife and I had this conversation the other night, as we spent some quiet post-Christmas time roaming the Internet from our respective laptops, a good five feet away from each other. There was a time, not long ago, that I just shook my head at the number of television sets we had in the house; now, for the three of us there are three computers, each allowing us to walk the road of the 21st century by ourselves.

What would we be amazed at, we wondered, 20 years ago? Would it be the Internet? The instant communication now available to us? DVDs? DVRs? DUIs (back to Britney for a moment)?

I thought about this for a while, reviewing the changes, and finally decided that back in 1988, if I'd been given a glimpse of the first few years of the 21st century I'd be most surprised by the George Foreman grill.

Not because of the actual grill, you understand, although I have one and I think it's a fine product. No, it's because I remember, as a young person, when that nice man on TV with the big smile, selling his cooking appliances, was a scowling, imposing fighter, a boxer who mixed it up with Ken Norton, Joe Frazier and

Muhammed Ali, winning the heavyweight championship twice, including as the oldest man ever to claim the title.

I suspect George would have been a little surprised, too.

In fact, boxing seems anachronistic in this century, although (or maybe because) it still exists in pretty much the same form. I admit to a fascination with the sweet science, a passion I discovered in the seventh grade and have never quite lost, although I don't bring it up in front of my wife.

It was also a passion for Norman Mailer, who didn't make it to 2008. I was never much of a reader of Mr. Mailer's work, although I still have a few copies. He was much more interesting to me as a character, a larger-than-life figure who blasted his way onto talk show sets, causing a ruckus and appearing, actually, sort of blasted himself. I wonder if we'll see that type of celebrity again, the full impact type who fights, philanders and faces down his demons, then goes home to write about it.

It wasn't, actually, a happy year for the writing community, as we lost several. Art Buchwald was a wit, and lived by them; in October 1942, at the age of 17, he found a drunk, bribed him with whiskey, and got him to sign as his legal guardian so that Buchwald could join the Marines. After World War II, he quickly became one of America's premiere humorists, oddly enough based in Paris for many years.

He wrote a weekly column that at its height ran in nearly 600 newspapers, wrote more than 30 books, and quite possibly had a brief affair with Marilyn Monroe. The end of his life seemed to amuse him as much as the rest of it, as he went home to die from kidney disease and managed to stay alive, writing his own eulogy while he waited. Goodnight, Mr. Buchwald.

We lost another newspaper columnist in Molly Ivins, like Mailer a character who seemed to stretch the boundaries of life. A Texan with impressive academic credentials, a fact she tended to smooth over with a drawl and some choice cuss words from time to time, Ivins made a mark in what was then a man's world, taking on politics, particularly the local variety, with vigor and relentless good humor. Molly I will miss.

Sidney Sheldon, Arthur Schlesinger, David Halberstam, Joel Siegel, Madeleine Engel, Ira Levin: I read and enjoyed them all, and we lost them all in 2007.

It was the passing of Kurt Vonnegut, though, that's on my mind today here in the past. There are Vonnegut works scattered throughout my messy house, collections and paperbacks and a couple of college library books I never got around to returning (I'm pretty sure I paid for them). His essays in particular I return to when I need a rhythm, a perspective or just a point of view.

I'll miss Kurt in 2008, and the others, but at least with writers we can always find them again, sitting on the shelves, waiting for the future to unnerve us enough to find solace in the written word. So here's to the future, to a new year, to the ones we left behind, to the books we haven't gotten around to reading yet but will, and should. And so, as they say, it goes.

(1/2/08)

14

The Numbers Game

I'd like to talk a little about what happened on May 5, 1945. If that date doesn't ring an historical bell, well, there's no reason it should. It's trivial, an oddity, but it's been on my mind lately.

But first we have to crunch some numbers.

In a way, numbers played a big part in 2004. From Iowa caucus votes to the number of people who saw more of Janet Jackson than they expected, to the amount of late night jokes about Howard Dean's "I Have a Scream" moment, from the increasing casualty count in Iraq to electoral math, from the counts against Martha Stewart to tenths of a point in Paul Hamm's Olympic victory, from the number of medals John Kerry won in Vietnam to the number of days George Bush spent fulfilling his National Guard duties, from the years between Red Sox championships to the hits that put Ichiro into the record book, from Bush's margin of victory in Ohio to King County's ballots, we were counting last year.

And sometimes re-counting, of course.

Now we have new numbers. Bad ones. Horrifying ones. For a solid week following Dec. 26, whether we turned on "The Today Show" or clicked on the AOL icon, we were greeted with a tally that held no good news. 24,000. 50,000. 100,000 and more, dead, crushed, drowned, swept out to sea in the tsunamis that roared across the Indian Ocean, reminding us once again that nature holds all the cards.

There can be a perverse comfort in these numbers, or if not comfort then reassurance that yes, we can believe our eyes, something bad has happened and it's big.

My daughter, who is 20, placed the numbers on the only scale she's known in a short life. "It's like ten 9/11s," she said at one point, and if that math is sadly deficient now at least I understand. There is no scale, after all, that makes any sense but still we try, so we look at the numbers.

And then we forget.

A friend e-mailed me the other day, a mass e-mail, informing us of ways we could help, in the form of donations. He mentioned that this might be the greatest natural disaster in our lifetime. He's a little older than I am. I appreciated the message and the need, but still I kept thinking of one word:

Bangladesh.

If you're older than 40, you know the word, even if the details are a little faint. In 1970, a combination of a cyclone and tsunami struck Bangladesh (then still part of Pakistan). The devastation was enormous; 266,000 lives were lost.

And in 1976 in northeastern China, an earthquake killed 240,000. Do you remember?

See, numbers are funny things. They become abstract, they lose meaning after a while, and then they disappear into history. Which may be simply a survival mechanism, a way of moving on.

There is truth to be found here, though, which is why I'm writing this. Natural disasters have occurred since the beginning of time: earthquakes, volcanoes, tsunamis, hurricanes, floods. And if you find a table of the biggest ones since recorded history, from the burning of Rome to the current tragedy, and you eyeball that a bit, you come up with an interesting figure.

That is, the number of deaths from natural disasters over millennia doesn't come close to 27 million.

Which would be the number of dead between 1914 and 1945, the two world wars. Nature is a pipsqueak compared to us when it comes to horror, a piker, second string. We do death better.

This brings me to May 5, 1945. I told you I'd get there.

In the last year of World War II, following Jimmy Doolittle's devastating raids on Tokyo, Japan launched hundreds of balloon bombs across the Pacific. These were filled with anti-personnel and incendiary devices. Most of them landed in the ocean. One actually made it as far as Michigan.

And one landed in the woods near Klamath Falls, Oregon, where six picnickers found it, dragged it out, and died when it exploded.

They would be, as it turned out, the only casualties on U.S. soil during that war.

Of course we've been hurt. We've seen death and destruction, both manmade and natural. But not our share. We've been fortunate, for different reasons, some geographical, some political, some cultural. Some just luck.

Luck is the ice patch that sends you slipping sideways without a scratch. Luck is your teenager turning the key in the door after midnight when you know somebody's child didn't make it home. Luck is a day without cable while your neighbor has a tree in his living room.

I'm not minimizing any suffering, please understand. In fact, I'm mostly just talking about me, sitting in my warm living room, knowing my friends and family are safe, watching devastation on the other side of the world and feeling fortunate. And wondering if good fortune, at least relatively speaking, carries with it some responsibility. I've been thinking that a lot lately.

The International Committee of the Red Cross and Operation USA are two places to go to help; there are others. What they really need now is money. It doesn't matter how much or how little you can give, either; in this case, there is strength in numbers.

(1/5/05)

Under The Weather

Writing about the weather in western Washington is only slightly less risky than trying to predict it. There are just too many variables. This is the meteorological equivalent, maybe, of rugged individualism; what happened at my house may not have happened at yours. So one has to be careful.

I do think we can all agree it was a little nippy there for a while.

And I had some snow, just a little. Again, maybe you did, too; I don't want to assume.

I like snow. I know that to some of you, this is like saying I enjoy traffic jams or flight delays, but it's my romantic side. When it snows, I remember my 3-year-old daughter, bundled up so tightly she could barely move her arms, trying to form a snowball. I remember the first house my wife and I lived in, 7000 feet above sea level in the mountains of northern Arizona, with six-foot drifts on the front lawn and a fire in the woodstove. I have nice memories of snow.

So I can get a little obsessive come winter. I watch the weather reports, looking for that magical combination of Arctic air and moist stuff. I'm almost always disappointed, but I got a little taste a couple of weeks ago, and it occurred to me then that maybe in addition to obsessing I get...I dunno. A little weird. I'll give you a couple of examples.

First, there's the snowman my neighbors made. I didn't see them do it, but it was a classic. Branches for arms, carrot for the nose, everything. It was, in fact, a very well-constructed snowman, the kind an engineer might build, which may very well be the case; these are new neighbors and I don't know them yet.

It's been a remarkably durable snowman. The snow on the lawn disappeared pretty quickly, but the snowman's hanging in there. Almost two weeks, as I write, and he's still looking good.

A little too good.

Snowmen melt ugly. They decompensate, they drip from the top down, like the Nazis in "Raiders of the Lost Ark" at the end. You want to turn your head and not think about that Frosty song.

But somehow, in this weather, this snowman is giving up the ghost gradually, and in a subtle way.

He's getting thinner.

It's like The Snowman Who Cut Carbs. The Snowman on the South Beach Diet. The Snowman Who Got Stapled. Or else he's got some sort of degenerative illness. Because I'm pretty sure he ain't been exercising.

It's really amazing. I'm almost tempted to walk up to him and say, "Man! You look great. What've you dropped, 50 pounds? You're a RAIL, a stick."

So I'm thinking maybe a few brain cells there got frostbitten. Maybe more than a few. I mean, you can contemplate a snowman's metabolism only so much before your local mental health professional starts taking copious notes and talking about lithium.

That's not the weirdest part, though.

As I said, I can get a little obsessive. Several times a day in the past week I was looking at the forecast, mostly because they kept talking about snow and that's all it was, talk. Talk is cheap, I say. I want to see results.

I'd look at one of those weather pages online, the ones with the extended seven-day forecast, with each day having a little box with a graphic: sun, clouds, rain, snowflakes. And underneath the picture would be two numbers, right on top of each other, the high and the low.

This confused me a little, although normally I'm not much of a weather watcher so maybe I don't know the right terms. But when it says the day's low will be 32 and it's currently 27, what's that about? So I was thinking, maybe they don't mean the traditional day, but the next 24 hours or something. Or maybe the overnight low for the next night. I spent a fair amount of time on this.

And then it occurred to me: They don't say "high and low" by the numbers. They don't even say "hi and lo." They just have these two numbers, one in red and one in blue. So it struck me that maybe I was looking at those numbers wrong. I thought, how do I know which one is supposed to be the low temperature and which is supposed to be the high?

I swear. I thought about that for maybe a minute.

Maybe you have to think about it for a minute, too.

Oh, well. It's back to wet and warm, same ol', same ol'. I seem to be a little more coherent, but it's still winter. I'll keep my eyes open for maybe one more snow, just so I can sit on the sofa and watch. In the meantime, though, I'm back to concentrating on my own waistline and staying away from weather reports, watching the gutters drain appropriately and making sure the roof doesn't leak. I'll be normal again, then, as much as that's possible.

But I might sneak another peek at the snowman. Just to make sure he's not jumping rope or something when I'm not looking.

(1/19/05)

Don't Rain on my Parade

My wife gave me one of those artificial sunlight lamps for Christmas, so now I'm pretty happy.

I'm not sure I was all that unhappy, or if I was if it had anything to do with dark days, but I work in a small home office in my basement, which being a basement is sort of underground, and at any rate it was a present from my wife so I'm just going to say I'm happy and leave it at that.

And my kids gave me one of those ionic air purifiers that supposedly sucks bacteria out of the environment. In case you sense a theme here.

I only mention the lamp because I wonder what friends of mine in Arizona would think. I spent 15 years of my life in Arizona, most of that in Phoenix, which they refer to as the Valley of Sun and for some pretty good reasons. I believe I read once that Phoenix averages 421 sunny days a year, which sounds about right. I'm guessing Seasonal Affective Disorder is not much of an issue.

It's different here, though, and lately we've been reminded of just how different it is, and we are. In the past couple of weeks a fair portion of America has been focused on the Pacific Northwest, since we had the audacity to go and get us a winning football team, and it's been interesting to see our area through different eyes.

Most articles I've read are complimentary, if sometimes in a back-handed way. We're literate, educated, opera-attending, theater-supporting, book-reading, coffee-drinking, mountain bike-riding, outdoor-loving, jaywalking-eschewing polite people, if a little distant. And damp.

One writer even used that word. He referred to us as "damp people." Personally I prefer to think of myself as moist, but everybody's got an opinion. And you can't blame them. Not only was Al Roker commenting on our nearly four straight weeks of rain, but the serious stuff showed up just in time for the national media and the Hawks-Redskins game, reinforcing the stereotype and (one can hope) discouraging Sun Belters from even thinking about moving up here and increasing the equity in our houses once again. It's crowded enough.

So if the rest of the country wants to imagine that we're soggy folks, addicted to caffeine and needing bright lights to stabilize our serotonin levels, I say let them.

But no more dissin' our Seahawks. That monkey's been shooed off our shoulders. We're heading for Motown with momentum. Time for a little respect.

Even people who don't follow football are talking about it. I hear it in the grocery store and the convenience store, on the radio and in lines at the bank. There are those more familiar with "The West Wing" than the West Coast offense now tossing out "Matt" and "Shaun" as if they were relatives who made good. It's sort of funny.

And nice, and overdue. Community is a relationship, after all, and though relationships are complicated things part of the glue that holds them together is a sense of shared passion, small or large, serious or trivial, long-lived or ephemeral. Regardless of what happens in Detroit on February 5, it will be over and fade and March will come and we'll move on, but if for a period of time we sense something in common, I think it's a good thing. And may our mothers forgive us, but sometimes it's just fun to talk to strangers.

So whether you've suffered for decades or hopped on the bandwagon in December, welcome, there's plenty of room. And pay no attention to those East Coast elites, the snobs and all the rest, the ones who sneer at the NFC West and already have their bets on Pittsburgh. I'll tell you why.

Years ago, in my very first newspaper column for Beacon Publishing, I was talking about optimism, and I picked the most cockeyed example of that I could think of at the time. Here's what I wrote:

"I believe the Seahawks will go to a Super Bowl in my lifetime."

So take it from me. Seattle 44, Pittsburgh 21. Call me crazy. Tell me I'm blinded by passion.

Tell me I'm all wet.

Because I am, sometimes, and so are you, and if a little water bothered us we wouldn't live here. That's another shared secret we have, something that goes without saying, something the rest of America will never understand.

Let's not tell them, either.

(1/25/06)

Where The Boys Are

Today, class, we're going to discuss that phenomenon of the past 30 years or so, commonly referred to as the Modern Married Man.

This will probably be on the test. Just FYI.

You know what I'm talking about. You can find him in the cities and the suburbs. He's as comfortable pushing a stroller as a lawnmower, maybe more so. He might bring home the bacon but he's probably perfectly capable of cooking it, too. He could change the oil but diapers aren't out of the question, either.

In other words, he's not your father's....well, he's not your father's father. He may not even resemble your father. Ward Cleaver would be scratching his head and looking at Wally and the Beav in a new light.

This isn't a role reversal as much as a blend, produced and sometimes necessitated by changing social structures and economics, not to mention a fair amount of enlightenment. Marriages have always been partnerships just as a matter of definition, but sometimes limited and there have been inequities. And there still are, and relationships are individual and personal, but in a general sense, at least in the Western world, we've seen some changes.

And yet. Speaking as a male-type person, I can assure you that, to use sociological terminology, boys will be boys. Studies have shown that women live longer than men in large part because men do really dumb things sometimes.

Again, I'm painting in broad strokes here, but I suspect that for a lot of men, our choice of a mate involves several factors, some of them maybe under the surface a little. In addition to mutual attraction, compatibility, shared values and goals, we might subconsciously at least be also looking for something of a moral rudder, an ethical complement to balance some of our darker impulses. In other words, it's sort of like getting a companion, partner, lover, and Jiminy Cricket all rolled into one.

So what happens when they go away?

What happens when, say, your wife has to leave town for a couple of weeks to attend a national board meeting of, I don't know, maybe something like the Presbyterian Association of Musicians? What happens to a 46-year-old man and a 15-year-old boy and a neurotic (also male) dog when a stabilizing force leaves them alone?

A friend of mine summed it up best, I think, a few years ago when his wife left him alone for a week or so.

"It's Pop-Tart time," he said.

I don't understand it, really I don't. Why is a man who is perfectly capable of making bread, a roast, soup from scratch and Chicken Kiev suddenly subsisting on one food group, i.e., Basic Dorm Room Cuisine. Why has the dishwasher, which theoretically is functional, suddenly become a decorative appliance only? How come I spent an hour on Sunday watching bass fishing on TV? Why is the dog suddenly finding lots of food on the floor to eat? And where did all the chocolate milk in the refrigerator come from?

Maybe there's a scientific explanation, some sort of reverse evolution. Maybe, given enough time in a testosterone-only environment, I'm going to start dragging my knuckles and developing a prominent forehead.

Okay, I'm exaggerating a little. Still, we spent Saturday afternoon watching all three "Austin Powers" movies and seeing who could burp the loudest. Even the dog was laughing a little. It just seems strange.

The truth of the matter is that after 22 years, I've grown accustomed to my wife being around, and it's been a little disorienting. You'd think after all this time it'd be nice to have a little time apart, but you'd be wrong.

25

There's no music in the house. My bed seems way too big. I'm drinking out of paper cups, light bulbs are mysteriously burning out, I keep misplacing my keys, and the towels in the bathroom don't smell all that good.

I'm not really complaining, just musing on the mysteries of men and women and marriage. What doesn't kill us makes us stronger, they say, so assuming we survive another week, and I expect we will, the boys will be better off. And if distance makes the heart grow fonder, then I suppose I'll become something of a romantic fool for a while, which has got to be a good thing.

Then my daughter can relax and stop calling me every day, wondering if we're still alive. The chocolate milk budget will decrease. I'm sure there are light bulbs around here somewhere, and if I concentrate I know I'll remember how to load the dishwasher soon. There will have been some male bonding, which we don't do enough lately, and I learned some interesting things about the new sorts of lures they have for bass fishing.

And late one night, I'll drive out to SeaTac to pick up my wife and my world will seem a little more normal. I for one will be very appreciative.

But right now I've got to go. I think I hear the pizza guy at the door.

(1/26/05)

Goodnight, Mr. C.

I decided to give it a week, just to see what, if anything, I had to say.

I don't have any anecdotes, after all. I never met him. I was never on the receiving end of his encouragement or generosity. He didn't change my life, as far as I know, or particularly influence the way I thought or what I wanted to do.

I was curious, though, from the moment I turned on the TV that late Sunday morning and saw that Johnny Carson had died. I watched the coverage off and on that day, until both the clips and Don Rickles began to get a little repetitive. Maybe it's because it's a Sunday, I thought, a slow news day, but I suspected something else.

As the remembrances and testimonials continued into the week, someone mentioned that it was as if a head of state had passed away. I tried to remember if the death of another show business personality had ever got as much attention and I came up empty. It seemed that a good part of America got a little wistful for a week.

And I wondered about that.

There are good reasons, of course, and we've heard them all by now. How his Midwestern roots endowed him with heartland sensibilities that appealed to all of us. How his ownership of "The Tonight Show" (first figurative and then, eventually, literal) and his personal passion kept the quality high over that amazing run. How, during tumultuous times, we waited to here Johnny's spin in that opening monologue, to laugh before bed and talk about the next day.

But as I listened to, and read, the reactions of ordinary people, people like me, people who never sat on the couch and joked with Ed and Doc, I sensed something else, and I finally realized that I was hearing "I grew up with Johnny Carson" a lot.

It makes sense, too. That big chunk of demographic, the Baby Boomers, would have been anywhere from teenagers to toddlers when he started on "Tonight," and while maybe their parents caught less of the show, sacrificing a few yuks for that 6am alarm and work the next day, a lot of us were night crawlers, at least in the summers and holidays, and Johnny owned the night.

It was that way for me, at any rate. Over the years, first as a teenager with a small black-and-white TV in my bedroom, then in college while I was supposed to be studying, or after the occasional swing shifts I worked in my 20s, I passed a lot of years with Mr. C.

The pictures that have been painted of this man in the past week or so are interesting, if only for the glimpse we get of a very private person who spent the last 13 years of his life out of the spotlight. We understand that he was painfully shy, uncomfortable in large groups or with strangers off the set. He battled booze, apparently. He was intelligent with a wide range of interests, including astronomy. He never lost his love of magic. He smoked like a chimney.

And, of course, he had that particular constellation of talents and traits that made him, simply, the best that ever did that peculiar job, and probably ever will.

Still, I wondered about all the fuss, and then realized the answer was there all the time, in my own house.

I went into my son's room that Sunday, sat on his bed, and told him the news. He sighed, hung his head a bit, and said, "Oh, no."

Think about this. He was born in 1990, two years before Carson left for good. How could he possibly know?

Because I taught him.

Ten years ago, for Father's Day my wife gave me a set of Carson tapes, collections of moments, monologues and skits. And a few years later, I passed them on to my son, just to see if he liked them.

He wore them out, literally. He thought, this then 10-year-old boy, that this was the funniest stuff he'd ever seen, even if it was thirty years old. I thought so, too, and now, suddenly, I know what I think.

I think we used to share a lot more, all of us, families and strangers. And even though, as today, we could be divided about politics and war, we had things in common, things we saw and heard. Now our choices are seemingly endless, so you have your show and I have mine, she has her music and he has his, I'm on the Internet and you're listening to your iPod and he's playing a video game and she's watching ESPN.

Choices are good, and change is inevitable, and there's no going back to 1975, anyway. But my son and I sat and laughed again together that day, watching the clips, and it occurred to me that there used to be more of that. A time when a lot of us laughed together, at the same moment, at the same things, up later than we should have been, unable to resist, knowing that going to bed with a smile is a good thing, knowing that millions of your neighbors were smiling, too.

(2/2/05)

Ready For Some...Something Else

I can have my moments, like any of you, I suppose, of over-inflated ego, self importance and imagined uniqueness, so it's my guess that most of us were feeling the same things a few days ago.

I was anxious, then optimistic. I was nervous and wary and hopeful and prayerful, and for a period of time over the weekend I was sleepless in Snohomish County. There were just so many intangibles. And finally I relaxed, relented, gave up and figured what would happen would happen, and it did and you know what? It's going to be all right.

My plum tree survived the great wind storm of 2006, and I have a little more time now to get around to cutting it down.

What? You thought I was talking about something else?

Perspective is the refuge of losers, someone once said. And maybe it was me; you write enough columns, you start repeating yourself. Certainly, also, Mr. Aesop understood something of human nature. Those Super Bowl grapes would probably have been sour anyway, knowing as we all do that the officiating was generally the worst performance since, well. Pick any Pauly Shore film.

It was an odd game, though, wasn't it? With a crowd estimated at 90% Steelers fans, Pittsburgh not only had a 12th man in the stands but a 13th in stripes. I sat through the whole thing, alternating between hope and disbelief. Not just at the bonehead calls, either. The Hawks played poorly. Pittsburgh actually played worse, but they had enough plays to come out on the winning side and it's wait 'til next year time.

And it's OK. If we've learned anything in the past week or so, it's that there are important things, and then there are more important things. An earthquake and the worst wind in years reminded us that Terrible Towels have nothing on Mother Nature.

Then there's New Orleans, still shattered from Katrina and then they got tornados. Maybe Pat Robertson has the answers there, but all I see is a mess that's years away, if ever, from getting unmessed.

And I guess I could mention the passings of Coretta Scott King, Betty Freidan, and Al "Grandpa Munster" Lewis. All lived fairly long lives and contributed to society, if in different (and in Al's case, weird) ways, but losing a loved one is never easy and families are grieving.

Sort of makes that play when Matt Hasselbeck tackled the defensive player who intercepted his pass and got called for an ILLEGAL BLOCK seem irrelevant. Or maybe it does. Maybe in a week or two.

I have a friend going through some marital problems from hell at the moment. It's hard to listen and not be able to help, but there's strength and determination there and these things happen. Still, it's enough to sort of make me forget that Steelers touchdown that EVERYBODY KNOWS REALLY WASN'T.

There's plenty of joy out there, too. A buddy of mine just signed a contract for his second book in as many years. My daughter seems awfully happy these days. I have three DVDs of "Northern Exposure" sitting on my desk, just waiting for me to revisit Joel and Maggie and all those quirky folks in Cecily, Alaska. I do believe I've seen a big yellow orb in the sky from time to time lately, too.

And then there's my plum tree, still standing (if tilting) where it belongs, which is anywhere but through the roof of my house.

So there's plenty of good stuff to help us forget the holding call that wasn't holding, which took the Seahawks from the 1-yard-line back to the 40. I guess.

And some of those commercials were really funny. The

Stones were, too, although not in, you know, a good way. Just my opinion.

We're moving on, in other words, and that's what we do. What are a few dropped passes and a couple of missed field goals in the big picture? Spring is coming, the grass is starting to grow, and our neighbors are peeking out of their winter homes, looking for their shadows and saying hello from time to time. I thought I heard a bird singing the other day, even.

So mighty Matt may have struck out, and there may have been a significant lack of joy in Mudville last Sunday, but we're a forward-looking group out here in the Northwest, and we can certainly put that idiotic offensive pass interference call into perspective. It's February, after all, and you know what that means.

Time for Mariners spring training.

See, don't you feel better already?

You don't really have to answer. It was a rhetorical question.

And didn't those Steelers fans in Detroit all look fat and drunk?

But I'm over it.

(2/8/06)

My Girl

If you're any sort of a movie fan, and I'm assuming you are or else I'd feel really dumb writing this column, you know that this Sunday, February 27, is Oscar Night.

So, if you're one of those like me who looks forward to the annual Academy Awards, and you're starting to get anxious about the winners and losers (and who doesn't?), I'm here to help. I'm giving you a head's up on who's taking home the statues. No need to thank me; my pleasure.

I'm actually the perfect person to pick the winners in advance, as I've only seen one of the nominated movies. This is a good thing, trust me, since Oscar predictions are usually based on three criteria:
1. Who SHOULD win.
2. Who WILL win.
3. Something else I can't think of at the moment.

This year, though, having little first-hand knowledge of the films involved (and thus no personal bias), I decided to approach it scientifically. The Oscars are voted on by individuals, and over the past decades there has been little, if any, scent of scandal or corruption, so we can first of all figure it's a clean race. Plus, it seems pretty easy; I don't think there's much chance of someone intending to vote for Leonardo DiCaprio for Best Actor, for example, and accidentally casting their ballot for Pat Buchanan. This will be a chad-free vote.

And, although these are individuals, a look at history gives us a sense of a group think mentality. After all, these are people in the same industry. So, after doing my usual exhaustive research, which frankly I don't think I get enough credit for, here are my predictions.

Best Supporting Actor: Morgan Freeman for "Million Dollar Baby."

Best Supporting Actress: Cate Blanchett for "The Aviator."

Best Actress: Hillary Swank for "Million Dollar Baby."
Best Actor: Jamie Foxx for "Ray."
Best Director: Martin Scorsese for "The Aviator."
Best Picture: "The Aviator."

There. Now you can relax and enjoy the show. I feel very confident about this. And please, someone let me know   if   I'm   right.

Because I'm going to miss the Oscars this year.

Oh, I might catch a little of the end, if it happens to run a little long (you think?). But I'll be otherwise engaged.

Sunday I'll be marking the 50th anniversary of an event that profoundly changed my life, as well as many other lives. I'll also be marking the 22nd anniversary of another day that changed my life, if in subtler ways.

Did you know we're re-living 1983 this year? Yep. Wonder what day of the week February 27 was in 1983? Just look at your calendar; same as 2005.

On that Sunday in 1983, I took my girlfriend to meet my parents.

They'd met her before, actually, briefly, back when she and I were just co-students in college and co-workers in a restaurant, but this was different, and I sensed they were dubious. I'd switched girlfriends in mid-stream, after all, and I'm sure they worried this would be a pattern, a bounce from love to love. Still, they were gracious and friendly.

And my mom had baked a cake. Because it was Julie's 28th birthday, that day, that Sunday, the one I remember so well.

My mom does things like that.

I bought her boots for that birthday. The next year I gave her a shower massage thing, but we were married by then. We still are.

We still are. I have no explanation, no sense of why she hasn't kicked my sorry rear out the door on many occasions, except that maybe everyone needs a project in life and I am hers, I dunno.

34

But after 22 years, I still like to lie on the bed and watch her stand in front of the closet in her underwear, trying to make a decision. I still perch at the top of the stairs and listen to her sing. I still, sometimes, sit on the sofa and watch for her out the window. I still want her to laugh at my jokes and eat what I cook, to read what I write and remind me to take a shower once in a while.

So Cate and Leo and the rest will have their shindig without me this year. I take what I can get, and what I got was brains, beauty and talent, all of it wrapped up in five and a half feet of Texas' Finest, and if I forget that once in a while then shame on me.

But not this Sunday, no sir. This is my girl's day, and she will have a good time, knowing she's at the height of her powers, knowing that life is just now getting very interesting. This beats the movies any day, but particularly this one, and the fortunate few who come away Sunday night with a little gold man will have nothing on me, nothing compared to what I'll be bringing home that night, knowing, as I do, that I wander through life bathed in the glow of reflected light, lucky man that I am.

(2/21/05)

Spring Clinging

Lent started last week, at least for Christians. For everybody else, it was just March.

Lent is an interesting concept, at least to me, a liturgical way of pointing out what we already knew, anyway: There's room for some improvement here, dude.

My wife loves Lent, I think. It's just the thing that gets her brain rolling in interesting theological ways. It's not about sacrifice, after all, not about spilling a little blood on the altar or cutting up your credit cards. It's about cleaning your closets and making room.

It's also not about you, if I understand my wife correctly. In other words, you can give up the cigs or the booze or the chocolate or the eBay or the fatty foods, and while that might be a healthy choice if on Easter morning you haven't changed the world in some way then just maybe you need to try harder.

Kind of daunting, I admit. And I gave some thought to the Lenten season. I was sort of intrigued by the "forty-something" aspect some people pick as a starting point. Walk 40 minutes a day? Drink 40 ounces of water daily? Write 40 e-mails to people I love and tell them how much? Get up every morning at 4:40 on the dot?

I ended up watching "The 40-Year-Old Virgin." But not because of Lent, just because I heard it was funny. And it was, although awfully vulgar. Not for the kiddies or the squeamish.

On the 12th day of Lent, my daughter is coming home for a visit and bringing The Man. This is how she used to refer to him when they first started dating, actually. The Man. His name is Cameron. He's a singer and plays jazz trombone. He grew up in San Antonio, Texas. His parents live in Santa Fe, New Mexico. He has a dog named Rosie, about whom he is unabashedly sentimental.

That's pretty much all I know. Except that he apparently loves my daughter, and my daughter loves him, and so now I finally get to meet him and we are cleaning our closets.

We're not only amazingly messy people, but we've lived in this house for 18 years and no one ever mentioned to us that we are now part of a throw-away culture. Sometimes I think Cameron should be given the unvarnished picture, that he too should have to step over baskets of laundry and push magazines and books out of the way to find a place to sit down and not look too closely at the bathroom, but we rarely have company and are sorely in need of a little spring cleaning. That's the goal, anyway.

I'm all in favor of small steps. I figure if we can get the dining room table so clean that you could almost eat off it, that might be enough. But I suspect I'm going to have to make more of an effort.

Truth be told, I like The Man already, for a couple of reasons. First, he sent us Christmas presents. Yeah, I made a sarcastic comment about him sucking up to the girlfriend's parents, but I saw my son open a Miles Davis CD and then I unwrapped two DVDs for my wife and me. The first was "Camelot," the film, a seminal subject in the history of my marriage, a college play that pushed my wife and me down a road that led here.

The second was the entire first season of "The Muppet Show." Which was a gift so stunning in its perceptiveness and whimsy that I got a little tongue-tied.

The second reason is more instinctual, but at the same time based in reality. See, I've seen a lot of pictures of the two of them. Candid, posed, goofy, funny. And there's one constant:

In every one, Beth is glowing.

Fatherhood ain't so hard. You do your best, you flail and you fail, you have some successes, and then you let go. You hope you haven't snarled their psyches too much, that they find forgiveness for your many faults as they get older, that they scoot through the rough patches with minimal trauma, and that some day they find a reflection in another person that makes sense.

There is so much room for improvement in my soul that I can get overwhelmed, but I've decided to let the season lead me, and I look forward to a visit, as always, from a red-haired girl. She may have found another man, someone else to cook for her and pick her up when the car breaks down, but then I always knew that would happen, anyway.

And if her time is limited, and most of it spent showing a Texas boy her Northwest roots, I understand that, too. I'll take what I can get and be grateful, and remember to look on the bright side.

At least I'll always have Kermit.

(1/8/06)

As The Crow Flies

I once wrote, thinking about the Iraq war, that it seemed so far away. In fact, I thought, you probably couldn't get further from my house than Baghdad without getting closer.

This wasn't a bad eyeball guess, I suppose, at least if you're a little fuzzy on spherical geometry and stick with the Northern Hemisphere. I do recall, though, from high school geography, that there is more than one hemisphere. At least two, I think.

Those of you who are more frequent flyers than I, and I'll stick to flying for this discussion (I assume swimming takes longer), and who've endured that marathon from Sea-Tac to Australia, probably are shaking your heads. And you're right.

In fact, Seattle to Sydney is 7739 miles, while Seattle to Baghdad is a mere 6813. My mistake.

But Australia isn't the winner. As it turns out, the furthest place from my house (again, only in airline terms) is Fort Dauphin, Madagascar, at a comfortable 10,778 miles. I don't know of any commercial airline that offers such a trip, although if there were I assume we'd have a one-hour layover in Denver.

The quickest way would be flying east, by the way, crossing the tip of Greenland, diving down through northern Europe and slipping along eastern Africa. Since the flight from Fort Dauphin east to Sydney is another 6000 miles, I'm pretty confident that Madagascar is the furthest. Enjoy your trip.

Yes, I wasted a lot of time on a website I found Saturday morning.

I do love my maps, staring at far off places and wondering what it's like there on the other side of the world. And it is. If you started digging in your backyard, straight down (get some friends to help you), you'd end up right in the middle of the Indian Ocean, probably a little east of Madagascar (you could dig to China, but you'd have to start in Argentina).

I don't know what the weather is like in Madagascar, although I assume it's warm. Sydney might be warm, too, although of course their summer is over and winter is only three months away there.

Which brings me, finally, to the point of this dumb column.

Did I miss winter?

I remember Christmas. I remember a couple of weeks of cold weather. Yes, now that I think about it, it snowed a little one day. But unless I hibernated for a few weeks and my wife didn't tell me because it was more pleasant around here, I think we skipped a season.

I mean, I went out shopping the last weekend in February and I got a sunburn. This is just strange.

I'm not complaining. I've enjoyed the weather as much as anyone else, driving with the windows open and the coat in the closet, even knowing as we all do that there is karma debt here in an early and endless spring. It can rain all April, May and June and we still won't be doing much lawn watering this summer.

Mostly, though, it reminds me that we live in a special place, tucked up here in our corner of the globe, protected by topography from most ravages of nature. We have wet and warm springs, glorious summers, crisp autumns and mild winters, and sometimes no winter at all. We certainly have fears and concerns (rising energy prices, drought, earthquakes, floods, Randy Johnson playing for the Yankees, others), but I don't know how any of us can spend a winter like this one and not feel a little fortunate to be where we are. At least when we look around and spin the globe a bit.

The tsunami, of course, a disaster that will be decades, probably, in its effects. Then there are the manmade issues: North Korea nukes, Russia, Iran. And Iraq.

Two springs ago, we saw perhaps hope in the toppling

of Saddam's statue and what felt like a quick war. And an election has been held now and there is still hope, ink-stained fingers hope, but it feels sluggish and slippery. We sense a long haul, a difficult time, perhaps an American presence for years. And there are now 1500 American names, 1500 stories and suffering families, 1500 who will see no more springs, 1500 who died in the desert while we went about our mild lives. And the thousands who have been injured, maimed, changed.

And the thousands who remain. These are the ones I'm thinking about today.

I'm not trying to be nobler than thou here. I certainly don't feel guilty for enjoying the nice weather; as far as I know, I have nothing to do with the weather. I just was reminded, sitting here, listening to birds sing and lawn mowers crank up, playing with some maps, that 6800 miles is still a long distance. And regardless of what you think of the war, whether you think it was a good idea or bad, there are friends and neighbors, family, teachers and doctors, far away, who will be seeing an entirely different spring this year, and it's not a stretch to imagine that most of them just want to come home.

(1/9/05)

Where Have You Gone, Joe DiMaggio?

Hearing the news about the latest Mars probe, and realizing I was barely paying attention, reminded me that we do tend to get jaded. Men walking on the moon? So 1970s. The Internet? Yawn. Cell phones, GPS navigation, mapping the human genome, high-definition television, those little pills that end heartburn: the stuff of science fiction, once upon a time, and now ordinary and everyday. Surely there'll be something soon, something new and futuristic, but I can't imagine what it'll be. Maybe time travel. Nobody's done that yet.

Well, maybe once.

"What's the greatest sports achievement of all time?" I asked a friend a while back. "Bob Beamon," he answered. I wanted to know why.

"Because you've asked me that same question probably a dozen times over the past 20 years." Sorry. I forget sometimes.

Bob Beamon was a long jumper from Jamaica, New York, a good athlete but certainly not the best jumper in the world. He made the U.S. Olympic team, though, and in the summer of 1968, in the running for a medal in his event at the Mexico City games, he took off, hit his mark, and soared into the 1990s.

The long jump record had been broken 13 times since 1901, on average by a total of about 2 inches. On that day in 1968, Bob Beamon traveled through time and broke it by almost two feet.

I've never heard a good explanation. He wasn't the best in the world; in fact, he never even came close to his record again. Yeah, it was thin air at a high elevation, but then why didn't another jumper do something similar? In fact, the rest of them stayed comfortably in 1968 while Beamon spent 10 seconds or so in the future.

It would take 23 years to surpass, most at that 1- and 2-inch pace, and Beamon seemed surprised as everybody else by his moment of flight and his leap into the records. It was an aberration but in an odd sport where, one imagines, given a unique sort of circumstances funny things might happen, if only once in a blue moon.

Sports records are usually more sedate, sliding along the continuum, pushing the barriers gently, and usually measured in inches, or centimeters, or seconds. Some are oddities, a moment when nature seems to bend a little. In 1961, for example, Mickey Mantle and Roger Maris ended up fighting each other and history for the Major League Baseball home run title, with Maris launching #61 and passing Babe Ruth in the record books. And while other hitters got close, it would take nearly 40 years to break.

Shattered, actually, by Mark McGuire and Sammy Sosa in 1998, something that made more than a few fans scratch their heads and wonder. Was it just time? Or training? Or something else?

And then we had Barry Bonds. Maybe there's something about alliterative names.

I'm not surprised at the new book by San Francisco reporters Lance Williams and Mark Fainaru-Wada ("Game of Shadows") outlining their evidence, apparently pretty good, that the most obnoxious athlete in professional sports took steroids. It did seem strange, the way he suddenly bulked up and started dancing with the future.

Well, it's only cheating.

But for a lot of us, and maybe most of us, I suspect, who've made serious mistakes and errors and committed sins of commission and omission, who've forgotten birthdays and sloughed off duties and given in to desires and dreams that might better off be put away for a while, cheating is the line we don't feel comfortable crossing.

A lot don't see the line, duh. They swindle and sell and

flim-flam and lie, but most of us can't go there. We can conveniently forget we owe money to family or friends, ignore the weeds, assume that the roof will hold another year and hope for the best, but we don't cheat except to assume that one day the air will be thin and we'll go a little further than might be expected by our past achievements.

And in all fairness, nothing's been definitively proved. Bonds denies using steroids. And sure, always a spectacular athlete, maybe he just got more spectacular suddenly.

It's just that I think you ought to grab destiny at the dust you find by the fireplace. Bread crumbs in the forest, yellow brick roads, old wardrobes in old rooms, swords stuck in stones, stars seen through primitive telescopes. Work, in other words, and chance and choices and determination, not drugs.

I suspect there's some minor league politician out there already, seeking to make a name for himself or herself, wanting to hold Barry Bonds in contempt of Congress for his testimony a year or so ago, claiming innocence, but then there are other lies to deal with, more important ones than who swung a bat and when and why and how it went so far.

I just was thinking of Roger Maris, and his kids and grandkids, and of Bob Beamon hitting his mark and taking off, not knowing where he would end up and not imagining how far he would go, but learning later that it was pretty far, and that it was all on the record.

(3/15/06)

44

Fun with Technology

I looked around the other day and thought of what I could live without, and I came up with a list.

A dishwasher is nice, but not necessary; I grew up without one and saw. The stove could break down, but with a microwave and my George Foreman grill (and Subway) we could survive if we had to.

For a family that watches a grand total of probably four hours of television a week, we have five sets, although four are pretty old. Still, we could lose three and not really notice.

Cell phones, cable, multiple CD players, the entire "I, Claudius" series on videotape: convenient, yes, but we'd probably be okay without them.

But I need my computer.

It's my livelihood, my connection, my communication source, the thing that gets me up in the morning and keeps me alive, along with oxygen and love and sandwiches. I really, really need my computer.

So last week I was on the phone, and I noticed my computer was shutting down. Since I normally have several programs running at once, this took a minute or so, and honestly I wasn't all that concerned. It's happened before, usually when an automatic update occurs and I don't catch the "Do you wish to restart your computer now?" message and it just figures (I guess) I'm busy and reboots by itself.

But it didn't start again, and I couldn't persuade it to. No flicker, no error message, no nothing. It was dead.

It's fairly new, and still under warranty, so I called tech support. You probably know the routine, and the limitless joy of this experience. First there's the music, the menu options, the waiting. Then there's a young person with more scripts than a telemarketer, probably sitting in the Bahamas somewhere, who instantly is on a first-name basis with me, something that took my wife two years.

"Chuck, my name is Dale. Chuck, this conversation might be recorded for monitoring purposes. How may I help you, Chuck?"

"First of all, Dale, have you ever heard the name Linda Tripp?"

"Pardon me, Chuck?"

"Never mind. A joke. Look. My computer was working fine, and then all of a sudden it shut down, and now it won't start up at all."

"I see, Chuck. One moment, please (clickclickclickclick). OK, Chuck. Is your computer on at this time?"

"No, AS I SAID, my computer won't start. It shut down and now it won't start again."

"One monent (clickclickclickclick). OK, Chuck, would you turn on your computer for me?"

Long, poignant pause.

"Dale, if I could turn on my computer why would I be talking to you?"

Short, clicky pause.

"OK, Chuck, so I understand your computer won't start. Now, first of all, I need you to exit all programs that are currently running…"

Little beads of blood were breaking out on my forehead.

"Chuck, is the power on at your house?"

"Chuck, is your computer currently plugged in?"

"Chuck, have you recently struck your computer with a hammer or another blunt object?"

Clickclickclickclick.

After an hour, or possibly a week, of going down the list of theoretical possibilities, Dale and I determined that my computer would not start. Thank God for the experts.

It was then, after hanging up, after wondering when I last backed up (last week? August?), after wondering how long it would take to move the other computer downstairs, after wondering how long it would take for my computer to get fixed, after wondering if I had ever deleted from my hard drive that cute picture I took last summer in the hotel room on our anniversary of my wife stepping out of the shower, after starting to disconnect things, that a theoretical possibility occurred to me.

It occurred to me then that it was theoretically possible to reach around the back of the computer and accidentally dislodge the power cable, but not enough to be noticeable, just enough to disconnect. And since I have a laptop, it was theoretically possible for the battery to continue to power my computer for two or three hours until, of course, it finally shut itself down.

It didn't need repairing. It just needed electricity.

I thought about calling tech support back, but then I had second thoughts. I had lots of thoughts, actually.

"Hi, just wanted to let you know I solved the problem. Thanks for your help."

Clickclickclickclick.

"Chuck, I understand your computer won't start, is that correct?"

"No. I mean, it wouldn't start but now it does, it was just a loose power cord and the battery ran out. Sort of an Occam's Razor thing, you know, the simplest solution is usually the right one, ha ha."

Clicky pause.

"So, you struck your computer with a razor, is that right, Chuck? Was this when you tripped over Linda?"

Bloody pause.

"Never mind. My computer is fine. Thanks anyway."

"OK, Chuck, please exit all programs for me."

Must stop writing. Blood in eyes. Strange urge. Urge to find hammer. Must resist.

Must delete picture now.

(3/16/05)

47

Looking Back, Forward

I write this particular column once a year, I think, although that's fairly easy to check and I don't want to. One of the down sides to writing a weekly column, along with the occasional hate mail and the fact that now everybody knows everything, is that it's impossible to avoid being redundant. I'm going to repeat myself, and sometimes in the same sentence, and that's just a fact.

So I apologize in advance for any inadvertent déjà vu. I've said this before. I will say it again. I can only hope somebody invents some more words pretty soon so I can add a twist or two.

It began this time in my e-mail box, as most things do. I find remarkable things there, although rarely something I'm looking for, which in most cases is either my debit card or my gloves. People send me stuff, as I'm sure people send you stuff. Links, articles, musings, motivational essays, prayers, poems and political philosophy that I may or may not agree with. Everybody wants to be helpful.

This one was one of those "magic" essays that float around the Information Superhighway, unencumbered by documentation or attribution. It could have been written by Harry Potter for all I know.

(More likely, it was written by somebody like me, who likes to get paid, and then hijacked, twisted, puffed up and posted all over. I can tell you horror stories of places I've found my work. Let's just say I was amazed to learn there's such a booming industry in the production of personal discipline products.).

It was about nostalgia, which I'm all for. I like looking back as much as the next guy (unless the next guy is interested in classic cars or, say, comic books, in which case I don't like it quite as much).

I have great affection, for example, for television shows of the 1960s and early 1970s. If I catch one of these on

TV, or watch a retrospective, I'm taken immediately back to my childhood, all warm and fuzzy, idyllic and innocent, surrounded by love and clothed in PJs.

This is nonsense, of course. I grew up in a time of incredible chaos, social unrest, an unpopular war and political assassinations, generational chasms and general divisiveness, and also? Most of those shows were really, really bad.

Try telling that to the writer of this piece I recently received, though. Not only did the author go on (and on) about the joys of life in black and white, he or she seemed intent on perpetuating a political/social philosophy that I have a hard time categorizing but I guess safely can call "moronic."

You've probably read things like this. "Hey, we rode our bikes all day without helmets, we ate raw meat, we could wander all over the neighborhood without cell phones to check in with our parents, and nobody died, right?"

Well, pardon me for blowing some sunshine up your skirt, but people died. And just the way surgeons eventually discovered that they could drastically improve the mortality rate of their patients by simply washing their hands, we learned about E. coli and that a cheap bike helmet could decrease childhood head injuries at a phenomenal rate. But try telling that to people who think the world has gone to hell in a hand basket.

The truth, I suspect, is that when we pine for what we remember as a simpler, quieter and better time, what we really miss is being children.

And we forget that things are better now.

There are plenty of examples of why we're better off, despite all of the problems that never seem to leave an era alone. We live longer. We have access to information at our fingertips. We understand more things, and we can fix problems faster. Fifty years ago, a diagnosis of cataracts meant cloudy vision and possibly blindness for the rest of your life. Today, it means about half an hour in the chair and, as a bonus, pretty near perfect vision out of the box. I, too, could go on and on.

But maybe (and here's where I've written this before, and before) we should just look at our black-and-white past for a second. Remember the film "Back To The Future"? A 1985 teenager rockets back to 1955, with its quaint morality and quiet neighborhoods. Wouldn't it be nice to live there again, with those nice picket fences and manicured lawns and functional families and classic TV? A world minus the noise of video games, cell phones going off every second, profanity-laced popular entertainment and rude waiters?

And the bomb shelters? And the "Whites Only" signs? Polio, anyone?

Sigh.

I don't mind wallowing in the past, really I don't. I just try to keep my perspective intact and my hands washed. And as bad as things can seem today (and they can seem bad), I can't help looking forward to some things getting better, as they tend to do. Call me optimistic, maybe, or idealistic, but while I walk down Memory Lane I also know my feet are going in one direction only. And that may not be such a bad direction, all in all, especially since I have a sneaking suspicion that where we're going, we won't need roads.

(1/23/08)

50

The Last Campaign

They all looked so innocent. People can be devious, though, and hide their secrets well.

It seemed like a good idea at the time. My wife and I decided to visit a church we hadn't attended in a few years, although for complicated reasons having nothing to do with the people there. So we went, and had a good time seeing old faces. There were handshakes and hugs, some close conversations about kids and careers, and somewhere along the line one of these good people played a little winter joke on me.

A few days later, the results of close contact were in. A tiny RNA virus of the Orthomyxoviridae variety had burrowed into my body, replicating at will and causing me to question the propriety of going to church on a day I could have been watching pre-game shows all morning.

OK, it was just the flu. But I didn't care for it at all.

I know many of you have been invaded yourselves this winter, so you understand. It was fairly straightforward; there were no sudden lurches to the bathroom, for example, or wadded-up tissues on the floor. A mild cough, a less mild sore throat, and a fever that hung around 102 for the better part of 48 hours, causing strange dreams and for one disquieting moment the inability to think of the word "moon."

I slept for 30 of those hours, tossing and turning, murmuring strange things and making the dog uncomfortable, as he apparently worried (with good reason) that I was suddenly capable of accidentally stepping on him in my delirium.

It passed, as these things tend to do, no real harm done, but I discovered I'd become a changed man. It was on Saturday night, actually, as I was still recuperating, managing just enough energy to sit down and turn on the TV, that I had an epiphany.

I was watching the news coverage of the South

Carolina Democratic primary, which Barack Obama won handily over Hillary Clinton and John Edwards. As I watched, I saw footage of Sen. Clinton's famous husband on a stage, waiting to be introduced, his mouth in that perpetual open "O" that seems to have replaced lip biting, pointing at people in the audience, and a remarkable thought occurred to me, which was:

If I never see Bill Clinton again, it will be too soon.

Some of you are nodding now. Stop that.

Seriously. Don't put me in that pool, that vocal minority of Americans who hate everything Clinton, who think he's the personification of all evil, the perpetrator of all manner of crimes, no misdemeanors. I was never like that.

I voted for him twice, actually, eyes wide open, and I have no regrets. He was a disappointment, ultimately, all potential and promise, all aborted by character holes big enough to drive a truck through. Still, it was a happy, prosperous time for many, including me, and after he left office, arguably one of the most popular presidents in recent history, I caught his appearances from time to time and still appreciated his good points. He was bright and articulate, insightful and occasionally even humorous, and he seemed to be doing good work around the world. And I heard his wife was keeping busy.

What happened this past week down south is so novel, so different from anything we've ever seen before in terms of presidential politics, that it's still difficult for me to pin down the moment I realized I was tired of Bill Clinton. Maybe it was just his overwhelming everywhere-ness. Maybe it was his distortions of Sen. Obama's statements. Maybe it was the sense of inevitability and even destiny that he and Hillary Clinton seemed to exude. Maybe it was the subtle (and not so subtle) racial code he injected into the debate.

And maybe it was just the flu.

But I wanted him to go away, and I wanted her to go

away with him. I wanted the 1990s to stay where they belong, the age of the psychodrama of Bill and Hillary to be over once and for all.

Again, this is coming from someone who finds a lot to admire in both of the Clintons, even given their shortcomings. And, in the spirit of full disclosure, from someone intrigued by Sen. Obama in many ways, and less than inspired by the current Republican crop of hopefuls.

And certainly Sen. Clinton is still the odds-on favorite to win the nomination.

But as I watched Barack Obama give his victory speech, once again fighting my inner cynic and my inner idealist, wary of his eloquence and admiring it at the same time, I couldn't help thinking that maybe Bill Clinton's last campaign would be a losing one.

And maybe for this reason: Clinton has been called, with good reason, the greatest politician of his time. I agree completely.

I just suspect that it's no longer his time.

(1/30/08)

The Losing Battle

I am Everyman. I know this because people tell me all the time. "You're Everyman," they say, which is a little disappointing since I've gone to great lengths to preserve my secret identity, the traumatic roots of my dual personality, the location of the Everycave, etc.

"Everyman," as we all recall from English literature class in the tenth grade, is the title of a 16th century morality play, translated from the original Flemish, "Elckerlijc," but try putting that on a business card.

It's come to represent an ordinary person with ordinary traits and habits, a baseline from which we all deviate occasionally but wish we hadn't, particularly the next morning. Normal, in other words, somebody the rest of us can relate to but not envy, since by definition Everyman is in every way and in every case ever so boring.

That would be me, according to the kind folks who stop me in the grocery store. Apparently I got this reputation for normalcy by writing in this column a lot about my family, my lawn, and my dog. People think I'm a normal person with a normal life, while those who actually know me are currently laughing so hard their stomachs hurt and they're spitting out food they ate a couple of weeks ago.

Oh, I'm sure I do the boring thing pretty well, but you would just have to walk inside my house (not that we would allow that sort of thing) or observe my family for, say, three minutes to reconsider your definition of "normal" and maybe think hard about calling 911.

There are still clothes in the dryer from 1992. There is dust that has been here so long it's developed a rudimentary civilization. There are areas of my backyard I haven't seen since the (first) Bush administration. I always need a haircut, my son moves furniture into the bathroom, my wife talks back to the TV, and I'm pretty sure the dog sees dead people.

Normalcy is, actually, something I crave from time to time, and even aspire to, which my neighbors try to encourage. But it's hard to pin down, and it keeps changing on us. It used to be normal for people to fill their gas tanks with change they found under the seat cushions, for example, or to go out in public without earphones.

Let's do a little experiment and try to create an Everyman, just for fun. He's 38, married, with two kids. He owns his own house, which he's refinanced twice. He's 5'10" and 170 pounds. He has light brown hair and green eyes. He makes $45,000 a year. He has two cars, one a late model and the other several years old. He has mild hay fever and a penicillin allergy (rash), but otherwise is in good health. He doesn't smoke and drinks only occasionally. He doesn't use illicit drugs, and what he did in college is nobody's business. Let's give him a nice haircut just to be fair.

Is he normal? Statistically speaking, I mean, in terms of averages and medians and other words I don't understand? Could we consider him pretty much Everyman?

Nope. He is strikingly, even remarkably abnormal, and I'll tell you why, although some of you already have figured it out. You know who you are.

No, this is an extraordinary man, at least in this country, by virtue of the fact that he is not fat.

That's right, America. You've suspected it and read about it and now you know it. Two-thirds of us are overweight, and that's without Marlon Brando around to skew the figures. Mr. Average up there is a minority, and by all indications it's going to get worse for him. Pretty soon he'll probably have to start shopping for clothes at specialty stores and paying extra for narrow airline seats.

So I guess I'm pretty normal after all. You too, maybe.

And once in a while, I want to feel special again. Unique, even. I resolve, I swear, I stay in the produce section, I start an exercise program, I cut carbs, I count calories, I watch fat, and I find myself at 10 o'clock at night searching the store for peanut butter and chocolate ice cream because I will die without it.

It's an awesome responsibility, being Everyman, and sometimes I wish this burden could be lifted, but we all have our jobs and maybe this is mine. The ordinary is calling me. Even now, as I write this, I can almost see the Every Signal in the sky, or hear the Every Phone ringing, summoning me to stay in the middle of the pack, to put on my sweat pants and extra-large shirt and venture out to do battle with the forces of evil.

Although it could just be the UPS guy. Maybe if I put a hat on he won't notice my hair.

(1/11/07)

Mission Statement

I hung up the phone and could almost hear the cameras begin to whirr, assuming cameras still whirr and given that, of course, I didn't actually "hang up" anything. There was a cinematic overlay, though, a narrative about to unfold. I was on a mission.

I picked my clothes carefully but casually; I would draw no attention today. I laced my shoes three times, facing down the Goldilocks dilemma – too loose, too tight, just right. I didn't need to be bending over at an inopportune time, or tripping. This was just too important.

With time to kill, I put some gas in the car and then checked the air pressure in the tires. The front driver's side needed a little inflating, and I was glad to do it.

I meandered to the mall, taking the back way but not conspicuously so, and stopped at the bank. It wasn't my branch, of course; there would be no nosy questions or casual conversation. I asked for cash, and I wasn't particular about the denominations; just make it legal tender, buddy.

Arriving at the Barnes and Nobles in Lynnwood, I backed into the parking space so I had an unobstructed view. Everything looked copasetic so far, but I didn't get to this advanced age by taking chances. I saw her before she saw me. She seemed a little harried, rushed and out of breath, but I knew this stranger and I knew she had what I wanted. She was reaching for her cell phone when I whispered the code word we'd agreed on.

"Mary," I said, although I'd never assume that was her real name. Or even the correct password, since our phone connection had been problematic and she had some sort of accent I couldn't verify. Then again, she was from Kirkland. Maybe they talk funny in Kirkland.

Our business was short and sweet. I handed over some pictures of dead Presidents and she gave me a box, no questions asked and no information offered. I walked

57

back to the car, trying to look nonchalant while my heart seemed poised to leap through my sternum and do a little break dancing on the pavement.

I made one call from the car, terse and to the point. "The eagle has landed," I said, and my wife sighed.

"So that's done," she said, and I headed home. I ruminated about stopping at the grocery store but dismissed that quickly; after all this, I wasn't entrusting my treasure to a few measly car locks.

I made it home, negotiating the front steps with my arms full, and it was only then, with my package securely stowed under the bed, that I really started to breathe again. Mission accomplished in true Tom Cruise fashion (I was picturing Bruce Willis, though, to tell the truth). I had done the deed, made it to the mountaintop, crossed the Rubicon and lived to tell the tale with my laces still tied.

I scored myself a Wii, man. And not a moment too soon.

A Wii, for those of you who don't know, and I assume there's a solid neurological reason for that, is Nintendo's latest offering in what is now the seventh iteration of video game systems. It came on the market in September 2007, although on looking back that seems sort of theoretical; demand outpaced supply enough to make Adam Smith's head spin, and that Christmas was rough for Wii seekers.

I waited, then, until February 2007, and on the morning of my son's 17th birthday I headed out to run some errands – get some gas, make a deposit, buy a Wii, pick up some milk and bread. The usual.

I walked into the game store and asked for a Wii, please. I can still hear the laughter, raucous and painful. I explained that it was my son's birthday, but these were cold and heartless geeks, and they had no Wii for me.

So I got an X-Box 360 and waited. Next year, I told myself. Surely it'll be easier by then. Surely, by then, I can just walk in the store and pick one up a few days before his birthday.

I think they were still laughing from 2007, or else they picked up where they left off as I walked through the door. Obviously, where a Wii is concerned, this is Bizarro Capitalism.

But I have an Internet connection and know how to use it, and after an hour of searching and leaving messages I got my phone call. I don't know how "Mary" came across her Wii and I didn't care, even if I could have deciphered her Kirkland accent. It came with a gift receipt and was unopened, and I gratefully paid 50 bucks above retail to see the look on my son's face on his 18th birthday.

His eyes widened and he said a few words, some of which can't be printed in a family newspaper but all of which were appropriate, given the fact that it was a Wii, and that I had managed to get one, and that I had used the very same words when I got home from Barnes and Nobles, sounding, in my mind, exactly like Bruce Willis.

(2/13/08)

Late Boomer Business

Boy, have I been irresponsible with this column. Here it is February, which means there are only nine months until it will be only nine months and then another three months and we'll have a presidential election. I apologize; time just got away from me.

So I want to talk about politics, but first I have mention a man who wore tights for a living. Trust me, this will all come together by the end.

I watched "Hollywoodland" the other night, a film about the last days of actor George Reeves. It was sort of light entertainment, well acted but lacking the dramatic weight I was looking for. Reeves was by all accounts a good actor, making his film debut in, of all things, "Gone With The Wind," but his nascent career got sidetracked by World War II and then the dissolution of the Hollywood studio system. The same thing happened to Ronald Reagan, actually, but Reagan had other talents and other passions. Reeves just wanted an acting career.

He ended up, in 1951, with Hobson's choice – it was either go back to digging holes for septic tanks or hold his nose for another reason. So he put on a cape and tights and became, for millions of little Americans, a hero.

This was "The Adventures of Superman," a low-budget show in the early days of television, and while it didn't make Reeves wealthy it did make him a star, at least to 6-year-olds. Sort of like Elmo.

It also made him typecast, a death sentence for a serious actor, and he eventually ended up, at age 45, dead of a gunshot wound to the head, apparently a suicide. There were some questions then and there are now regarding the circumstances of his death, and "Hollywoodland" wanders a little around this, but essentially what we have is a sad story, apparently a nice and talented man who never achieved his dream and never stopped dreaming. In the big picture, you could say that George Reeves was a bit player.

Unless you were talking to somebody like me, in which case them's fightin' words.

"Superman" actually went off the air around the time I was born, but it was rerun often in the afternoons when I was a small boy, and if anything I was more passionate than the kids a few years older than I who had waited a week for the new episodes. If you believe my mother (and she makes stuff up all the time), I spent a fair amount of my childhood with a red towel stuffed under my shirt and an odd appreciation of phone booths.

One of the producers of "Hollywoodland" made a comment in an interview that got me thinking, itself something of a superhuman feat. He made the point that George Reeves often mused that he'd be happier if he just knew one of his many fans was an adult.

And now we all are, as it turns out. Adults. Which brings me to Barack Obama.

(See? I told you. Don't blame me if my transitions are seamless.)

The junior senator formally announced his candidacy for the presidency last week in Springfield, Illinois, deliberately invoking our 16th president but also implying our 35th. I lost count of the times Sen. Obama used the word "generation" but the Kennedy connection was lost on nobody.

And if Barack Obama envisions himself as the leader of this "new generation," I have some questions. Since he's talking about me.

Who said, "He's dead, Jim"?

How about "Atomic batteries to power, turbines to speed"?

What does the phrase "muskrat love" mean to you? Or "afternoon delight"?

Do you know all the steps to The Hustle? If the

61

answer is "no," please explain why not (use the back of this page if necessary).

See, all this "generation" talk is serious stuff. It implies uniqueness, a shared experience that separates a group from the rest of the population. Those of us who, like Obama, are late boomers had no Vietnam to avoid, no draft cards to burn, no sit-ins to sit in, and no Woodstock to attend, separating us from our elder boomer brothers and sisters. In fact, it's hard to find a social cause or political figure that caused much of a ruckus for us, at least in that generational generalization way we use as shorthand.

What we do share is a culture, as goofy and silly as much of it seems now, and I wonder if Sen. Obama, having lived out of the country for a portion of his childhood, really is one of us. Not to take anything away from his intelligence, talent, passion and charm, all good and positive qualities. I'm just curious about what, if anything, he knows about kryptonite.

It just would make me more comfortable, somehow. I don't think it has anything to do with his qualifications for the presidency, and even if we're roughly the same age I'm not going to hold him to impossible standards. I don't expect him to leap tall buildings in a single bound.

But it would be nice if, like many of us, he once believed in someone who could.

(2/14/07)

Rob

Quick: What were you doing eight years ago?

Yeah. Me, too. It takes a minute to rewind our analog memories, and a lot of frames get dropped from attrition or insignificance. Eight years ago – let's see. I was 40. It was 1999, and all the talk was of the impending Y2K disaster when planes would fall out of the sky and Ross and Rachel would never hook up.

Other than that, my memory is pretty fuzzy. Eight years is nothing, a flip of calendar pages, at my age. Another eight will probably fly by, too.

It's different for young people. In 2015, when my daughter will be 30 and my son 25, I'm sure they'll look back at the past eight years as eventful and life changing.

As will Robert Pennington, although his story will be different.

I wrote about Lance Corporal Pennington last year. He was a member of what came to be called the Camp Pendleton Eight, seven Marines and one corpsman charged in the unlawful death of an Iraqi citizen. I came to the story by way of a friend, a former neighbor of the Penningtons who had watched Rob grow up.

I was suspicious back then. The whole thing smelled bad, with conflicting stories and hints of forced confessions, manipulation and political scapegoating.

I had no inside information, of course, and I still don't. I just know that Pennington has pleaded guilty to the charges of kidnapping and conspiracy, and was sentenced to eight years in the brig. As to how this will play out, and how long he might actually be incarcerated, I have no idea.

And it's possible he copped a plea, avoiding a murder charge, when he is truly innocent. People do that. Reading his words, though, I have to assume he did the deed, participated in the murder of an innocent Iraqi and then the attempted cover-up. I have to assume that military justice prevailed in its sad but necessary duty.

And I have to assume that my feeble imagination isn't up to the task of grasping the horrors Robert Pennington saw, the frustration and fear he felt, the living nightmare that was Fallujah, the heat, the paranoia, the loneliness, the anger, the exhaustion and the disorientation that must have come and stayed, after three tours.

The closest I come to fear is when I have to slam on the brakes or get my cholesterol checked. So I have nothing to offer here in terms of perspective.

But Rob Pennington is my daughter's age, and I have feelings about his generation.

I like them a lot. I know it's a raw generalization, but I like these 20-somethings. They offer me help in the computer store and serve me sandwiches. I've watched some of them grow up, and I get the sense that they're special, somehow. Recent polls, asking for their thoughts on various issues of the day, have given me hope. We might have a chance with this group, we just might.

They've grown up with diversity and tolerance is second nature, not worth thinking about. They want to make a difference in the world. They have remarkably close relationships with their parents.

And they hate this freaking war.

We're responsible, you know. I don't care how many peace marches you participated in, how many letters you wrote, how much money you gave to Gore or Kerry or how many chads you carefully disengaged. If you squealed for the first time in a delivery room within our borders, or studied our constitution and took your test, you put your name on the actions of his republic for better or worse.

This is the worse part. In case you were wondering what I thought.

It's not worse because we were frightened into an

unnecessary war, although I believe that. It's not worse because the rest of the world looks at us as if we were a deranged super hero, although that's true. It's not worse because the incompetents who got us into this ignored warnings and predictions about the aftermath and the need for more troops, etc., although God knows that happened.

It's worse because private citizens have to send body armor in order to protect our children. It's worse because VA hospitals are spilling over with wounded, walking and not. It's worse because veterans' benefits are being cut as casualties mount.

It's worse because another generation now has scar tissue, while we cluck over nonbinding resolutions and call radio shows.

Robert Pennington should be in college, or walking the beat as a cop or guarding our borders, not sitting in a cell for a crime he shouldn't have had the opportunity to consider. None of us can change that, not now. And we can argue from now until Tuesday about whether or not invading Iraq was a good thing or a bad thing.

What we can do is what responsible people always do, and that is clean up the mess. We can express our outrage that Rob's buddies still in Iraq don't have the supplies they need to stay as safe as possible. We can tie up phone lines and overload email servers to let our elected representatives know that wounded veterans don't just need care, they need the best care in the world, even if that means a few members of Congress have to skip Hawaii this year.

We can take care of our children now, and save the arguments for a quieter time. Maybe in eight years or so, when we can more casually discuss the merits of foreign policy.

God, I hate this freaking war, too.

(2/21/07)

65

The Root Of All Something

In an increasingly narrow-casted world, full of niches and specialties and various home improvement shows, one of the hardest things about writing a newspaper column is finding common experiences to which we can all relate.   After you get past the Big Three (love, parenting, and Anna Nicole Smith), we tend to scatter all over the place in terms of what we think, see, hear and care about.

We don't watch the same shows, listen to the same music, work the same hours, or eat the same food. We certainly aren't of a single mind when it comes to politics, sports, sex, food or recreational activities.   In other words, not only do I not know what you did last summer, I have no idea what you did last night, either. I'm just saying – it makes my job difficult.

So I'm always glad to run across something that seems to have legs in terms of cultural connections, and the Internet is a big one. I may have never seen "Law and Order" and you may not have a clue as to who Alton Brown is, but most of us have email and so we know about offers from Nigerian exiles and all sorts of fascinating products to spice up our love lives.

Some of you may even have received an email that resembles the following: "Cn yu rd ths? Th mnd s a fny thng; it fls in th gps whn lttrs r msing."

Maybe some of you are also thinking what I thought when I read something similar, which was ALL OF MY EMAIL LOOKS LIKE THIS.

Here's another psychological teaser.   Read the following 10 words quickly: Tree, bough, root, branch, leaves, water, stream, lake, canal, river.

How do you feel? Having pleasant thoughts of nature? Or have you suddenly developed an uneasiness, perhaps a disturbing sensation of dread? Do you know why? Of course you don't, unless you're a trained psychologist or

66

a newspaper columnist who had a bad weekend.

You're feeling uncomfortable because you've just read a line that, among other things, contains the words "root" and "canal." Your brain subconsciously registered this and started making plans to go out of town. Isn't this fun?

But enough about you.

It started as an ache on the right side of my jaw, but after a day or so I localized it to one particular tooth, which was tender if I did certain things (i.e., breathing and/or thinking). Still, it was manageable, and I even waited an extra day because my dentist's office was double booked. Not a big deal.

The x-ray was negative, but sometimes pictures lie, so after some probing and questions Dr. K started a process with which I have unfortunate but exhaustive experience, namely numbing my mouth. As (I believe) Socrates first observed, application of local anesthetic is never an indication of pleasant events to follow.

I need to mention that I have no dental horror stories to speak of. Dr. K and her fine staff work very hard to ensure as painless an experience as possible, and this has almost always been the case. Sure, there was that one time when an overzealous dental hygienist decided to overstep her authority and I believe actually extracted and then replaced several of my teeth, but I think they fired her.

When my "bough river" (for your sake) was done, Dr. K seemed surprised, but only a little, that sensation had already returned to my mouth. Sometimes a lot of bacteria can interfere with anesthetic, and maybe I had a lot of bacteria. It's not like I've been licking garbage cans, but I do forget to floss a lot.

So she gave me some Marcaine to go, sent me off with an antibiotic prescription, and told me not to be a stranger. It took me five minutes to drive to the pharmacy, and halfway there I was getting sore. By the time I handed over that script, I was in pain. By the time I got home, another 10 minutes, I was seeing double.

Another 10 minutes and I was yanking business cards out of my wallet, looking for Dr. K's number or possibly Dr. Kevorkian's. According to my wife, my skin had turned a shade that would make an albino shake his head in wonder.

I spent another 90 minutes in the chair while Dr. K did everything in her power to dull my nerves short of turning on C-SPAN, but this was a renegade tooth that had apparently gone over to the dark side of the Force, so my weekend was shot. I had to cancel my ballroom dancing lesson and everything.

I'm better now (thanks for asking), and I guess I've learned a universal truth: Pain plays no favorites, and maybe we're all linked by the fact that we're human, vulnerable and weak. Also, flossing is a good idea.

And sometimes relief is best found within ourselves. Taking deep breaths, making conscious contact with a higher power, and thinking of pleasant things. Green grass, the shade of a big tree, a gentle rolling river nearby.

Although I'm pretty sure I've ruined that image now for all of us. Me and my big mouth.

(3/7/07)

Final Goodbyes

There's nothing like hopping out of bed bright and early on Christmas morning, turning on some holiday music, making a hot cup of cocoa, lighting a fire, and realizing that no one else in the house will be awake for six hours to make one realize that things have changed.

Finding out that James Brown, The Godfather of Soul, had passed away at age 73 was a hint, too. We all seem to be moving in one direction.

I had no particular passion for Mr. Brown, rest his soul, although that had nothing to do with his talent and everything to do with my odd taste in music, so no anecdotes leapt to mind when I heard the sad news.

It did get me thinking, though, of those famous people who will populate the various "in memoriam" pages here as we wrap up 2006. Take Shelley Winters, who died this past summer. There's a famous (if possibly apocryphal) story of Ms. Winters being asked in her later years to audition for a film role, which comes in various versions but always ends with her pulling her Oscars out of a bag and setting them on a table.

There's another one I like better, though. She's walking into a building when she's greeted by a man coming out the door. When she has trouble placing him, he says, "It's me, Tony." Pause. "You know. I used to be your husband."

That would be Anthony Franciosa, who also died this year, within a week of his former, forgetful wife. He was the guest artist in a production of "The Rainmaker" in the 1970s at the university I attended, and I remember his fellow actors, all college students, being a little taken aback when they found out he shaved his chest rather than appear shirtless with gray hair.

Actor Glenn Ford also passed away in 2006, and I

remember reading about an incident when he was in location in Japan, filming "Sayonara" with Marlon Brando. Apparently Ford had his favorite cookies shipped in from the States, and when he found some missing he falsely accused his co-star of taking them. A few days later, spotting Mr. Ford's newly-arrived cookie package in the dressing room, Brando unwrapped them, set them on the floor, stomped them into crumbs, and then carefully replaced them in the package.

It's funny what you remember when the celebrity obituaries come out, the little ways these people we never knew or even met insinuate themselves into our consciousness, leaving us with sort of vicarious memories.

And, as in all years, we've lost some famous names in 2006. Ed Bradley. Milton Friedman. Mike Douglas. Peter Boyle. All accomplished, all successful, all leaving this world with a prominent mark or two left behind, worthy of a mention on the news or in the paper.

I started wondering, though, as I waited for my family to straggle out of bed on Christmas morning, about the not-so-famous who left us this year. So I looked some up.

Hey, it's called the Internet. Use it or lose it.

Bruce Peterson was an aeronautical engineer who put theory into practice, becoming a NASA test pilot and earning an unfortunate (in his opinion) place in television history. On May 10, 1967, during a glide flight of a lifting body Northrop M2-F, Peterson had a serious, and spectacular, crash landing that injured him severely. He recovered, although he was irritated that the footage of his crash was so stunning that it was used every week in the opening of "The Six Million Dollar Man." Bruce Peterson died after a long illness at the age of 72.

Mike Evans was one of the creators of the hit '70s show, "Good Times," but his moment in the spotlight came when he played Lionel Jefferson on "All In The Family," a young African-American neighbor of Archie Bunker who diffused and illuminated the older character's bigotry with humor and intelligence. Mike Evans died of throat cancer at 57.

Lamar Hunt (72) gave us the Super Bowl (the name, I mean). Mickey Spillane (88) gave us Mike Hammer, Red (89) Auerbach gave us Bill Russell and the amazing Boston Celtics, Freddy Fender (69) gave us "Wasted Days and Wasted Nights," and Red Buttons, Jack Warden, Barnard Hughes and June Allyson gave us hours of big screen pleasure.

And Elizabeth Bolden, who died this month at the age of 116, the oldest person on the planet, gave us a remarkable 562 (count 'em) living descendants, including 75 4th-great-grandchildren (i.e., the great-grandchildren of her great-grandchildren).

But even Ms. Bolden has to take a back seat to Harriet, who went to a better place this year after a staggering 175 years of life, having been born in 1830 in the Galapagos Islands, and a reputed (there's some question) associate of Charles Darwin himself.

Harriet was a tortoise, of course, which explains her longevity, but it's still a life worth noting, as are they all. So here's to life, and long journeys and accomplishment; and to new year, a short and mild winter, and an early spring.

By which time I assume my family will be up. Although I'm not holding my breath or anything.

(12/27/06)

Spring

"A little Madness in the Spring Is wholesome even for the King."

--Emily Dickinson

"To shorten winter, borrow some money due in spring."

--W. J. Vogel

"Lent is an interesting concept, at least to me, a liturgical way of pointing out what we already knew, anyway: There's room for some improvement here, dude. "

--*Spring Clinging*, page 34

For Every Thing, There Is A (Probably Non-Deductible) Season

The signs of the season are upon us. The heat gets turned down, the lawnmowers get tuned up, chocolate bunnies miraculously appear on grocery store shelves, and Ichiro steps out of the dugout, tugs on his shoulder, and looks for his shadow. Spring is here.

Spring is full of good stuff, but also other stuff. First, though, I want you to do a little exercise with me. Drive around your neighborhood (put down the paper first, I'll wait) and look for signs of entrepreneurship. C'mon, they're all around. House painters, drywall installers, lawn care people, daycare operators. You've noticed them, little placards on front lawns or painted sides of vans.

Politicians like to praise these brave, industrious dreamers, lumping them all together as "small business owners," the backbone of our economy, the palpable evidence that The American Dream is alive and well. The IRS simply calls them "sole proprietors."

The IRS LOVES sole proprietors.

So, if you have any springtime sympathy at all, you might extend it to these people, because along with rain and green things and warm weather comes April 15th. Tax Day. Coming up soon, too. In case you hadn't noticed.

As someone who has not only freelanced for most of his adult life but been married to a woman who's done the same thing, I know all about April 15th. In our peculiar yet loveable tax system, home ownership, childbearing and paying out the wazoo for health insurance are all rewarded, yet starting your own business with your own sweat and tears is not. I don't pretend to understand this, but to this day I can't pass a couple of kids selling

74

lemonade in front of their house without having to seriously resist the urge to roll down the window and shout, "INCORPORATE! TRUST ME!"

I'll explain how it works. Let's say you start your own business, out of your home. You get a client and a project, and let's say you (eventually) end up with a check for $500. What do you do?

IN THEORY: You earmark a hundred bucks or so for a special account that makes quarterly income tax estimated payments to the IRS.

IN REALITY: You buy food.

So April 15th can hold some surprises, none of them pleasant. Been there, done that.

This year was good, though. We even filed early, and electronically, and I discovered the other day that some nice IRS person had deposited a tax refund directly into my checking account. I keep going back to my bank statement and looking at it. It just doesn't seem right. It feels like pretend money. I'm going to let it sit there for a while just in case the federal government decides to take it back. Better safe than sorry.

One good thing about the uncertain life of self-employment is that it tends to force frugality as a matter of necessity; it's really the only thing you can count on. And it makes sense. So what if you don't make that trip to Hawaii this year? Hawaii will probably still be there, waiting. If you don't pay your PUD bill, electricity will one day disappear and you will realize that you miss it. Priorities, then.

I also learned to avoid credit cards whenever possible, for a couple of reasons. First, chances are with a little work I can always find a cheaper loan if I need one. Secondly, I'm a guy. As much as I hate to perpetuate stereotypes, my feeling is that if you send a guy out to get milk with an empty credit card in his wallet, he's liable to come home with a plasma TV. And then he'll need some accessories and a home theater system, and before you know it he's gone over his limit, just by a tad, which causes the credit card companies to break out the champagne and bump him to an interest rate that used to only be charged by guys named Vinnie who used your kneecaps as collateral.

I mention this only because recently, while staring at that IRS refund on my statement, I decided to check on a credit card of mine. I recently had used it and then paid it off, but with charges and fees you can never be quite sure. And, in fact, there still was a bit of a balance. There was no payment due, of course, no minimum, but I didn't just fall off the turnip truck and I paid it in full.

So on my next bank statement, I not only get to look once again at my theoretical tax refund sitting in my checking account, but also a payment to Mr. MasterCard for the grand total of 89 cents.

Which wouldn't have bought a plasma TV anyway, although it might have covered a cold drink from a neighborhood lemonade stand, even given inflation.

But kids, listen up. Hang onto your receipts. It can get ugly out there.

(4/12/06)

Eight Other Rules

I've never been a normal man, and now I guess it's too late to hope, but still I do. See, I think there's a fine line between being unique, eccentric, and weird, and I might have crossed it.

It's not that I'm miserable or anything. My wife knew I wasn't normal when she married me. My kids adjusted. The dog doesn't know any better.

Still, I can get a little wistful for normalcy. Not that I want to traffic in stereotypes, but it seems to me that normal men build stuff, fix stuff, hunt stuff, and burp, and I'm just no good at any of that.

My daughter discovered this a few years ago, when she was a teenager and certain male-type people started hanging around, ringing my doorbell or calling my phone or (in one instance) sending slightly off-color and suggestive instant messages to her, which I know about because I read one.

Beth would get very serious in these situations, and plead with me. "Please, Daddy, be nice to him when he comes over, OK? You can be so intimidating."

She was just projecting, of course, trying to conjure up a sitcom dad where none existed, but I made an effort for her sake. I practiced growling and muttering. I took to wearing my tool belt at all times and murmuring about running some conduit. I drank milk right out of the carton, picked my nose, scratched in public, and went to tractor pulls. I did mental exercises to conjure up long-lost memories of when I was an adolescent and just exactly what I was thinking about when it came to the opposite sex, which is not a fun exercise when you have a daughter. I really, really tried, but I couldn't pull it off, so finally we had to have a little talk.

"Look, Beth," I said. "The truth is, I really don't dislike these boys you date. Actually, most of them seem pretty decent and interesting. As for the rest, I just don't really care, as much as I know you want me to."

To her credit, she managed to avoid a crestfallen look and just nodded. As I say, she learned a long time ago that I wasn't normal. Still, she grasped for a straw.

"But don't you feel SOMETHING?"

"Yes. I feel sorry for them."

And I did, too. I'd look out the window and see one of these guys pull into the driveway to take my daughter to the movies or a party or the prom, and sympathy would be the emotion of the moment.

"Fresh meat," I'd think, shaking my head sadly, and wander off to drink some more milk. I couldn't help it. My daughter ate boys for breakfast. It was like watching an execution.

Bruce Cameron, a Colorado columnist for the Rocky Mountain News, once wrote a piece about fathers, daughters, and dating, creating The Dream Column. You never know. He called it "Eight Simple Rules for Dating my Teenage Daughter," and it evolved into a best-selling book and then a TV series that killed John Ritter.

Mr. Cameron seems to be a normal man, with normal feelings and a normal daughter. I, on the other hand, met my daughter when she was approximately one second old and knew immediately I was in trouble. She exited the womb with attitude. Talk about intimidating.

Beth lives in Texas now, 2000 miles away, and her love life is her own business, as it should be. It's a relief, actually. I hate wearing that tool belt.

Still, on the off chance that a potential daughter date discovers this column, I thought I'd steal from Bruce Cameron a bit and list my own eight rules. Which are...

1. Run.
2. Don't blame me.
3. Don't blame her mother, either.
4. Don't offer to arm wrestle. She's played the cello since the fifth grade. It will be humiliating.
5. Don't talk politics unless you agree absolutely with

her. She doesn't suffer fools easily.

6. Don't try telling her she's beautiful, talented, or brilliant. She knows this.

7. Don't attempt to persuade her to change her mind. She will exercise her woman's prerogative but only on her timetable. It would be a mistake, like driving into a tornado. Best not.

8. Did I mention not arm wrestling? Get her to tell the story of the church youth group trip when the boys were trying to impress each other by seeing how far they could throw a football. She had never held a football. Get her to tell the story.

And, if you're smart, even if your favorite movie is "The Godfather," you'll tell her it's "The Goodbye Girl." You might buy her a chocolate shake, too. Trust me on this.

And you might, if you have some sense of time and history, mention to her that once a 26-year-old man showed her Seattle at daybreak for the very first time. You might mention that now, almost 21 years later, he will still wander the house, waiting for her. That he loves her, and misses her. That he knows there will be other men in her life, and he wishes them all well, and he's glad to be out of the picture, but not all that glad, and not all that abnormal, as it turns out.

(4/13/05)

Patti O.

It was the hat I noticed first, thinking back.

It was colorful and bright, maybe purple. But it was a hat.

I used to sulk a little in church. I wasn't sure I really wanted to be there. I'd had some bad experiences with churches in my past, and I tended to enter them with a high degree of suspicion. I didn't really want to be there, but I felt I should. My family was there all the time, after all. So I went, but sometimes I just observed.

And as I watched my wife's choir come marching out, ready to sing, I noticed this woman with the hat. I have nothing against hats; I wear one all the time. And certainly hats in church aren't out of the question. Still, I wondered.

I eventually figured it out. I was a little naive back then. I hadn't spent any time with people undergoing chemotherapy.

I have since. It happens.

Her name was Patti Omiecinski, although everyone simply called her Patti O. She sat next to me at a wedding once and we had our first conversation, and she talked a bit about her recent bout with breast cancer. She seemed pretty matter of fact about it, which also was new to me, but she was friendly and good company as we watched young people take their vows.

I got over my church phobia eventually, and Patti and I ended up working together with the youth. For me, this was sort of like the blind leading the blind, but Patti O. seemed to be one of those people who had a natural affinity for teenagers, and I just tried to stay out of the way and learn something.

She was the kind of person who occasionally gets celebrated but mostly just serves communities in quiet, anonymous ways. Along with her church work, she was actively concerned about the least among us, the hungry and the sick without proper medical care. She was a nurse by profession and a nurturer by nature.

And she was always involved with the schools. After listening to me gripe once about a committee attempting to re-map our school district, she patiently explained how such decisions came about, and the hard choices that had to be made. Having herself been on a similar committee in the past. She opened my eyes a bit.

She wasn't a particularly tall or big woman, but she had a presence that could fill a room upon making an entrance, and then there was the smile. Patti O. had a great smile.

The twists and turns of personal relationships always fascinate me, particularly watching how pieces fall together over the years and interact. When Patti and her husband, Curt, moved to the Seattle area 20-odd years ago, they were welcomed and befriended by Dave and Janet Eaton (Dave and Curt were colleagues). Janet and Patti became good friends, and when the Omiecinskis moved up to Snohomish County, the Eatons looked around, saw something they liked, and followed them up here.

Lucas Eaton, then three years old, would eventually grow up to become one of my daughter's best friends. And Patti became something of a mentor to my daughter, leading a small group of young women in a study group. My Beth loved Patti O., and I think the feeling was mutual.

You can find connections in lots of things if you look hard enough.

Patti and Curt moved to Pennsylvania a few years ago, leaving Janet desolate and a big hole in the community. My wife and I had lunch with the Omiecinskis at some point before that, and while we weren't close friends we still had a great time. They were fun and interesting people, and I was sorry to see them go. And, as I said, Patti had this great smile. It made you want to smile

81

with her.

I stay in touch with Janet Eaton, sometimes just catching up with what our respective kids are up to, Beth in Texas and Lucas spending the past year in Europe. And sometimes we talk about other things.

It was Janet who told me, months ago, that Patti O. had gotten sick again, another type of cancer. It was bad news, but we knew Patti was a fighter. Everybody knew that.

Patti Omiecinski died in her sleep on Sunday morning, May 21, having lost her final battle, the one we all lose eventually. Some of you who read this paper knew her, remember her, and maybe haven't heard, and I thought you'd want to.

I was surprised. Not by the news, which was expected, but by the fact that as I read the e-mail the words suddenly became awfully blurry.

See, like a lot of people I sometimes find myself just loafing through life, not making much of a difference, letting the days slip by without thinking about them all that much. And sometimes we need to be reminded by someone, despite the difficulties that life throws at all of us, some harder than others, who knows how to live fully. Joyfully. Serving others, with bright, striking colors and a smile that lights up the room.

Which pretty much describes Patti O, and always did, and now always will.

(5/24/06)

Rest, Rise, Repeat

Dough called me the other day, out of the blue.

"Dude. Long time. Wassup?"

Dough is 22.

I spent a couple of years baking bread, rolls, pizzas, calzone — if I could roll it, knead it, proof it and deflate it, I was doing it. And then I stopped eating it, sort of, and just lost interest. I had other issues, too.

For a while, though, it not only kept me busy, fed my family and covered the kitchen floor with flour, but it sort of defined me. I became the bread baker to some people, particularly church people, who tasted my bread at Sunday morning communion. I got lots of compliments, which was nice, but it always seemed like a big deal over a small thing.

People have been making bread for a long time, and for good reasons: It's cheap, easy and filling, if nutritionally suspect (these days, anyway). Still, people would marvel over my remarkable ability to do something that essentially requires the motor skills of a 4-year-old, and maybe a measuring cup (maybe). People are funny.

I never minded the attention, actually, even as misguided as it was. Most of my cooking falls into the functional category; no one is lining up to try my tuna sandwiches, in other words. As for the rest of my skill set, it pretty much consists of typing pretty fast and doing a passable John Wayne imitation. I can manage to put oil in the car, mow the lawn, let the dog out, navigate the Internet, use a debit card and brush my teeth without breaking anything on a good day, but I'm not actually a natural tool user.

I also don't paint, sketch, sculpt, design, sing, dance, compose or take good photographs. Really, I assume the only reason you're reading this column is because your cheeseburger isn't ready yet.

But I can bake bread, sort of, and the other day I got

the notion, and it turns out I'm better at it. Baking has always been about patience and measuring, solid attributes for anybody, and not my strong points, but I seem to be getting a little better at that as I age gracelessly.

So I melted butter on low heat, brought the milk up to lukewarminess, sprinkled the yeast on top and gave it some space. When it bubbled and smelled just right, I mixed and kneaded and waited.

Baking bread, done properly, is a four-hour job, all but 20 minutes or so spent waiting. And I seem to do waiting now, so I let that dough get a good first rise, took it down a notch, split it in two, let it rise again, and we got some really excellent bread. Country white, with milk and butter and lots of sugar and honey, an insulin reaction waiting to happen. No good can come of bread like this but of course it does.

And after that, having found a rhythm, I made myself a pizza, stretching that rich dough over my knuckles until I got the right thinness, and man. It had pepperoni and mozzarella and jalapeños, and I ate several slices and then went to wrap up the leftovers and I ate them, too.

This was indulgence on my part, letting myself wallow in my late winter whatever. It's been ugly outside this season, cold and wet; someone from another part of the country would question me pointing that out, but you guys know what I mean. This winter just felt different, harsher and less fun, and then we have politics and strikes and scandals and banks going belly up. Good news was hard to find, so I decided to bake my own.

And now it's spring, finally, and I do believe I see some sun. The grass is whispering to me, I have more wardrobe options, and my neighbors have been poking their heads out of the house lately, either looking for their shadows or just appreciating the smell of newness. Looks like we made it.

But it took some carbohydrates for this guy, and while

it didn't necessarily elevate my mood it didn't hurt. Do no harm is the rule here, and although my pancreas might argue with that it felt like an accomplishment. I'd kept ennui at arm's length another night, and I learned another lesson. Sometimes it's not enough just to eat, get some nourishment and stoke the fire. Sometimes you have to get proactive. Sometimes, somehow, pizza just tastes better when you go out and kill the cheese yourself, and this one did, and I might make another one tonight, too.

(3/26/08)

This Old House

Like me, it's seen better days. Middle-age can be coy, sneaky and subtle, but it means business and we both feel it these days. Neither of us looks that great in the morning, for example.

I wasn't sure I wanted to buy a house, and I was very sure I didn't know how. I was 29, and the jolt of adulthood was just starting to settle down. I was beginning to enjoy some stability -- a baby daughter, a nice rented condo in Seattle, a walk to work. Home ownership was off my radar, something for a vague and distant future, some place in my life falling between getting new tires and death. Something for older people to do.

I would note, particularly to young people, that this feeling has never quite gone away. There are times even now when I'll be doing something responsible, surrounded by men and women my own age, and I have to resist the temptation to whisper, "Where are the grownups?"

So I blame my wife. This is easier than it sounds.

I worked downtown but her job was in Edmonds, so we looked north to Snohomish County, even in the 1980s having been priced out of the Seattle market. We made one half-hearted offer on a house in foreclosure, and then our realtor took us here.

The builder bought an undeveloped lot, mostly trees, and moved an early 60s rambler onto it. Then he jacked it up, built a basement, added some bumps here and there to the existing house, and ran out of money. We showed up one day, offered him $10,000 less than the asking price on a whim, and were mildly surprised when he accepted.

That was 19 years ago. I'm still sort of surprised.

Moving day coincided with nearly every able-bodied

male-type person I knew being out of town, so it was interesting. It ended at around 10 p.m., when I pulled the moving van into my new driveway and started to unload. There are a variety of ways to meet new neighbors. This one, maybe not so good.

Do people still do this? Stay in the first house they buy, I mean, the one they can barely afford, the one they bring babies home from the hospital to, the one that's supposed to be only the beginning and ends up being home?

We didn't know we were lucky. We had no way to know housing prices would start to soar in less than a year, effectively leaving us renters for the foreseeable future had we waited. We just wanted some place to live.

The following summer, my in-laws came out for a visit. My wife's father, noting the dearth of shade on the south side, took some trimmings from innocent trees and planted them in my yard. Most succumbed to absent-minded mowing, but one remains, towering over my house, an evergreen we call "Jimmie's Tree" but might as well be the Tree of Life, for life is what it's seen. There is detritus of nearly two decades, books and bikes, broken furniture, optimistic exercise equipment, and youth that never quite learned to get out of the way of time. In another 10 years, I will have lived here half of my life, and it shows.

I wander around sometimes, kicking ghosts out of my way and remembering dreams that never came to pass. The basement never got a pool table, or a wood-burning stove. The third bathroom never happened. Tiles never got laid, framing never went up, windows never got replaced.

But stir up enough dust and the memories leap out of cardboard boxes. My children grew up here, and left their marks. Funny how a stray crayon can take my breath away, after all these years.

There are problems, for sure. Roof issues. A back deck

being summoned by gravity. A swing set that I haven't gotten around to taking down, useless, only one rusty swing left.

We're going to stay, we've decided, fix what we can and live with the rest, because this is where we belong, or at least where we ended up, and there are worse things than staying in one place. In 16 months, I'll turn 50 in this house, and wonder if I ever could have been 29, but for the time being I'm content to remember.

I sit on that drooping deck sometimes, tempting fate, and look around. I can see my father-in-law's tree, tall and solid, as he is. I notice, in a forgotten corner of the yard, a boy's bike leaning against a bush, abandoned one summer day a long time ago and never retrieved. And sometimes the wind will pick up and set that squeaky swing into reluctant motion, and sometimes I will just sit there and watch.

(3/28/07)

The Other Chuck

Funny; I've almost written about him here in the past couple of weeks. Just as an anecdote, an analogy, a segue into more serious things, but there it is.

The subject at that time was Jeremiah Wright, Barack Obama's former pastor who was caught on the Internet with his rhetorical pants down, snippets of a sermon turned into chat fodder. Rev. Wright, as I'm sure you know, was videotaped saying, "Not God BLESS America. God DAMN America," and the talking heads shook with a righteous indignation.

Never mind that "righteous indignation" was exactly what Rev. Wright was talking about. And never mind that, when you read the transcript of that sermon, or watch the whole thing and not just the seconds shown, for a while, every 10 minutes on cable news, it starts to come across as a little ho-hum. Just another preacher, if a lively one, saying that America has some things to answer for. Jerry Falwell did this stuff all the time.

But that's another topic; what interested me was the visceral reaction many people had, jerking their knees at what sounded at first to be inappropriate and even blasphemous (not to mention unpatriotic). A clergyman using foul language in church?

Of course, it's not really foul language, just literal. That was Charlton Heston's argument, too, forty years ago on the set of a film, which is what is on my mind and only took me five paragraphs to get to, thank you very much.

It was "Planet of the Apes," and while I hate to spoil endings I'm guessing I can go ahead and tell you that it has a surprise ending. That is, after spending a couple of hours fighting a simian population on what he thinks is another planet, Mr. Heston's astronaut character discovers a shattered Statue of Liberty, instantly realizing that he was, in fact, on a future earth where some cataclysmic event had taken place. He (and we) assumed it was a nuclear war (it was the 1960s), and he pounded on the beach and screamed at the foolish people who had carelessly destroyed civilization, thus setting up an interesting evolutionary reaction and a seminal science fiction film (it's good, too; watch it sometime).

At any rate, the script called for him to use the "GD" phrase, as we're apparently calling it now, and there were some concerns about the language (how quaint) and Heston argued that he was literally calling on God to condemn, and eventually it was left in the film but sort of slurred and muffled.

Sheesh. No wonder I never have enough room to write.

Charlton Heston passed away last weekend, of course, at the age of 83, having been diagnosed six years ago with Alzheimer's disease. I wrote about this back in 2002, finding myself sort of inexplicably saddened by the news of his illness, and I knew why.

He wasn't my favorite actor, certainly. I actually found him sort of stiff and pedestrian, although I understand he was occasionally marvelous on the stage. He made appearances in a couple of my favorite films ("Apes" and Orson Welles' classic film noir, "Touch of Evil," released the year I was born), and he certainly was on the screen a lot while I was growing up, but I can't say I was a big fan. I've never made it all the way through "Ben-Hur," for example.

But Mr. Heston kept a journal from early on, and in 1978 he released it as a book. It was called "An Actor's Life," and my brother gave it to me as a gift, as I was thinking about being an actor back then. So I got familiar with his story.

It was an anomaly, actually. As the Hollywood studio system dissembled in the 1950s, Charlton Heston managed to carve out a remarkable 20-year career as a working actor. And he worked, moving from film to film, many of them the epics that were popular in that era, then the disaster flicks of the 1970s, interspersed with some Shakespeare, Westerns and historical films, and then he almost single-handedly legitimized the genre of science fiction in cinema by making several films that raked in the big bucks ("Omega Man" and "Soylent Green" to name two, in addition to the monkey business).

When his career finally floundered, he concentrated on stage work and smaller projects, lent his famous face and voice in various cameos, and became most prominent as a spokesperson for political causes, chiefly as head of the NRA for several years. He seemed cranky at times, and a little theatrical and vain, what with the toupee and the talk of "tyranny" and the sarcasm, but as I read over reminiscences this past weekend I see that even his political enemies regarded him as a decent and good man, remarkably polite and a teller of wonderful stories.

One of his most familiar concerned the chariot race in "Ben-Hur." His stunt coordinator tried to assuage his concerns. "Just stay on the chariot," he said. "I guarantee you'll win the damn race."

And I think, all in all, that he did, too.

(4/9/08)

Daughter Dialing

We're now far enough into the new millennium, five or six years (depending on whether or not you can count), that we can discern some patterns. Rules for living in the 21st century, maybe.

For example, if you're in the mood to make racial/ethnic slurs, make sure your plans for the day do not include being (a) at a comedy club, (b) at a political rally, (c) on your nationally syndicated radio show, or (d) under arrest.

You should also be cautious about casting your vote correctly, singing the national anthem with a live mike, preserving your most intimate moments on videotape, testifying before a grand jury, telling a joke when you have no sense of humor, and starting a war. And if you plan on going out in public, for God's sake make sure you have underwear on.

Also, don't lie to Oprah.

And now we have a new lesson: Be careful when leaving voice mail messages for your kids. Better yet, don't buy them a phone in the first place; you're just asking for trouble.

Most of the world, apparently, has now heard actor Alec Baldwin doing a little cross-country parenting via voicemail. In a message left on April 11, an obviously frustrated Baldwin scolded his 11-year-old daughter Ireland for not answering an apparently prearranged phone call, griped a bit about feeling foolish for interrupting his day to make the effort, used a few bad words, and ended by calling her "A rude, thoughtless little pig."

It's the "pig" part that seems to be causing all the commotion. To a lot of people, calling your child a "pig" is crossing the line. Take out the pig and you pretty much just have a father losing his temper. Add it, and suddenly all the talk is about mean daddies and scarred daughters, and Dr. Phil is volunteering his services.

And nobody seems to have ever had kids.

I remember when my daughter was Ireland Baldwin's age. She's 22 now, but it seems only a moment ago that she was 11. In fact, I can still see her in my dreams, usually manifested as a giant head that does nothing but roll its eyes and scream, "What's WRONG with you?" before it stalks off to the bedroom to watch "X-Files."

I also remember my wife, around this time, taking our daughter to the doctor, convinced that she was suffering from some mental disorder that required therapy or medication, and possibly boarding school. The pediatrician just smiled, though, and gently tried to reassure my wife.

"Your daughter is possessed by demons," she said.

Or that's what I remember, anyway.

My father would have been stunned by this. "Pig" would have been a term of endearment when talking about his adolescent son, hair down to my shoulders, sleeping until noon on Saturdays, a perpetual sneer on my face. I can think of other terms.

Alec Baldwin was being a jerk, of course, and I welcome him into the fraternity of fathers who lose it. I don't condone him or defend him, but I sure as hell understand him.

I was enraged at my daughter on a daily basis when she was about this age. Somehow overnight the Barbie dolls disappeared and she became infatuated with her newfound skill at sarcasm. She hated her mother and thought I was an idiot, subjects she could elaborate on in great detail.

I admit that I didn't handle it well. Words were said, feet were stomped, doors were slammed, and one time, now part of family lore, I got so angry I swung around from the kitchen sink, screamed something unintelligible, and hurled a slightly damp dish towel in her general direction. I just hope she doesn't write a book about me.

Maybe Alec Baldwin has anger problems; I can't say. Maybe he was just having a bad day, in an ongoing and messy custody battle with his ex-wife, and unfortunately took it out on his child. Maybe, as we venture through another wave of public voyeurism, his career has been irreparably damaged (although if "The Cat In The Hat" didn't do it, I have a feeling this won't).

I don't know if little Miss Baldwin was being thoughtless and rude, but regardless I suspect her self-esteem will hold up despite some name calling from Daddy (I can't vouch for other things, but hey – I didn't name her Ireland). I also suspect she and her father will work things out, because that's what families tend to do.

I like to think I have a good relationship with my daughter now, even after some rough years. And sure, even through the bad times, and even given the fact that I saw what the inside of her bedroom looked like, I have to admit that I never once called her a pig.

But I'm pretty sure that, from time to time, I was thinking it.

(5/2/07)

Big League

My father was a latch-key kid, before that term was coined, before the metacultural era when everything seemed to be about us and how our lives were so different. The combination of technology, shifting sociology and a whole bunch of baby boomers let us navel gaze to our heart's content, conveniently ignoring the fact that there have always been children, and some of them have always had to fend for themselves.

He was the eldest child of a single mother, and so sometimes he slipped through the cracks. He was shuttled, in the 1940s, between relatives and foster families, and what he remembered of his childhood (and he didn't remember much) was mostly loneliness, wandering streets, sitting on trains, wishing for stability and relying, often, on the kindness of strangers.

He would muse on this, sometimes, and on how he was fortunate to have grown up in his particular time (he could be metacultural, too), when he was safer than he would have been a few decades later, or so he thought. I'd call him on this sometimes, argue that there have always been pedophiles and perverts, monsters in our midst, and he'd agree but qualify.

"People were better back then," he'd say. "They took care of each other."

I don't know if this is true, or have the slightest idea of how one would prove or disprove it. I can only look at potential causes: Agriculture moved to industrial, rural moved to urban, community moved, maybe, to a closed circuit. Maybe we became self-contained, isolated, independent creatures who forgot how to socialize, and if that's the case then it's surely getting worse. If I want pizza and a movie on a Saturday night, just as an example, I can have them with virtually no human interaction. Add enough of those moments up and maybe we get a dysfunctional society; as I said, I have no way of knowing.

But maybe that's why we crave stories like the one I'm about to share. Maybe we always have, and maybe we just like to be reminded.

You might have heard it already; it has a local flavor, and even though there's been some national exposure it might resonate a little more here in the Northwest. I'm going to tell it anyway.

Sara Tucholsky is 5'2 and probably isn't ever going to be any taller. As such, the senior right fielder on Western Oregon University's women's softball team didn't hit for power, just placement, and with a batting average of .153 that wasn't a sure thing, either. But as she came up to bat the last weekend of April in Ellensburg, in a crucial game against Central Washington, two players on base in the second inning, luck and timing came together in one glorious moment.

The ball sailed over the fence, Sara's first home run ever, and as the crowd and her teammates erupted she watched the ball disappear as she rounded first base. Whoops. Missed the bag there, Sara. She stopped, turned to go back, and ended her college career with a twinge.

The anterior cruciate ligament, bane to athletes of all sizes, picked that moment to tear, and Sara crawled back to first while the crowd scratched their collective heads. Is there a rule for this?"

It's baseball. Of COURSE there's a rule.

If a player is substituted, it becomes a two-run single. If she's assisted by her teammates around the bases, it's illegal and an out.

If she's assisted by members of the opposing team, it's a national story.

You can probably finish this one yourselves.

The picture of two CWU Wildcats carrying Sara around the diamond, stopping carefully to touch her foot to each base, doesn't do the story justice. Nor does the coda, the fact that Western Oregon won the game and went on to the playoffs.

Nor, really, does the video clip of Sara telling her story, or Mallory Holtman, the greatest softball player in the history of CWU, the all-time conference leader in home runs, who came up with the idea of helping her injured opponent.

For me, anyway, it was the image of Gary Frederick, the Central coach for 40 years, now age 70, tears streaming down his face, talking on ESPN about his players.

Frederick reminded me of my dad, actually; about the same age group, growing up in the same era, the same beefy face and gray hair. My dad would have liked this story a lot.

And I infer nothing from it, no commentary on society at large, no silver lining in dark clouds, no glimpses of goodness in contemporary humanity. It could have happened anywhere, at any time, I'm sure.

But it happened in Ellensburg in April, a reminder maybe, a good story at any rate, and an answer for Tom Hanks's surly coach in "A League Of Their Own," who said, "There's no crying in baseball!" There is.

(5/7/08)

97

The iWar Generation

He would have been 90 this Tuesday, an old man. We can try to imagine him that way — white-haired, waving from a boat deck, leaning on a cane, talking with Larry King — but it's ultimately futile, a fantasy overshadowed by fact. He remains, instead, a figure in grainy footage, preserved by a trick of historical light. John Kennedy will always be young.

We don't think of him as a member of the Greatest Generation, of course, any more than we like to acknowledge that Willie Mays is 73 or that habeas corpus isn't the law of the land anymore. Like the late Kurt Vonnegut's Billy Pilgrim, he seems not frozen but unstuck in time, floating through contemporary American history, ready to be plucked by politicians needing the right attitude, or gesture or rhetoric.

Being Kennedyesque is the ultimate attribute, the Holy Grail of the modern political personality. Get the perfect hair, practice the smile, jab the finger some, slip in a New England vowel if you can get away with it, look young, act young, talk about energy and light and toss in a touch of the poet from time to time.

Barack Obama is the latest entry in the JFK sweepstakes. On Feb. 10, announcing his candidacy for president in Springfield, Ill., Obama invoked Abraham Lincoln but evoked the New Frontier, using the word "generation" a dozen times. "Let us be the generation ... " was his refrain, begging the question: What generation, exactly, would that be?

With Kennedy, we knew. When he said "a torch has been passed to a new generation," it wasn't a talking point, hustled through a dozen focus groups ("Should it be 'baton' instead of 'torch'?"). It was just a statement of fact, pointing out that the MacArthurs and Eisenhowers, the Roosevelts and Churchills, were Old Guard, remnants of the 19th century, and a new sheriff was in town. Kennedy had been to war, and then he had come home, and 43 seemed plenty old enough to be president after that.

That was the year, 1961, that Sen. Obama was born in Honolulu, a member of what social commentator Jonathan Pontell identifies as Generation Jones (roughly 1954-1965), a "lost" generation between early Baby Boomers and Gen X-ers.

I'm a Joneser, too, so I can tell you who we are. For most of us, if we remember John Kennedy at all, it's probably because there were no cartoons on the Saturday morning after his murder. While our older brothers and sisters were experimenting with sex, drugs and rock and roll, we were listening to "The Monkees" and learning to love the Big Mac.

We missed "Sesame Street" by a few years and "The Graduate" would have been incomprehensible had our parents allowed us to see it, but we had Mary Poppins and Butch Cassidy, and Adam West will always be the only Batman in our hearts. The Vietnam War (and the draft) ended while we were still in high school. Our college campuses were quiet, and by the time Saddam Hussein invaded Kuwait, most of us were raising families and settling into our 30s.

We did not go to war, in other words.

Our children did.

Born into Ronald Reagan's America, reaching adolescence with start-ups and soaring markets, traumatized by Columbine, stunned by 9/11, members of the Internet Generation or Cellphone Generation or File Sharing Generation have added another demographic asterisk to their résumés: They have their very own war.

Iraq and Afghanistan are Generation Y wars, fought in large part by young people who grew up in peaceful, prosperous times with accepted and expected futures, all of that suddenly jolted into perspective by the terror of

99

Sept. 11, 2001. They enlisted then, many of them, and the rest watched via technology that had become second nature, waiting for their friends to come home.

I freely admit my personal bias. I have a 22-year-old daughter, outgoing and friendly, so for years the house was filled with her contemporaries, with music and laughter and cellphones going off every 30 seconds. It was either get to know them or turn into an old coot, grumbling about taxes and yelling at the neighbor kids to get off my lawn, so I became an observer.

I like them, these 20-somethings who wander through my life, serving me sandwiches, renting me videos, selling me computer accessories and politely asking me if I know what kind of Web browser I use. They populate my wife's college classes, where she teaches them about art and music and they show her how to text message.

They seem genetically bred for a chaotic world, a generation of multitaskers, comfortable with doing a dozen things at once, all of them involving electronics. They appear to navigate life serenely, ear buds in place, alone with their music and connected at the same time to everybody they ever met.

They may, in fact, be the most cohesive generation on the planet, constantly in touch with friends, family and former first-grade classmates who contacted them via Facebook just to say hey.

And so they know about this war in an intimate way. They read blogs and e-mails from the other side of the world. They talk to parents of friends who serve, they exchange news, they post their own thoughts on their own Web sites. They see war by Webcam. Some of them will mark Memorial Day by remembering not fathers or uncles, but classmates. Brothers and sisters.

The war will end. They all do, sooner or later, more or less. When that happens, in whatever fashion — redeployment, staged withdrawal, etc. — families will be reunited, jobs will be returned to, wounds will be tended and colleges attended, and the future will once again begin to be imagined.

And the ones who went to war will have something to say about it. Like Kennedy's generation, albeit in much smaller numbers, the ones who volunteered, who wanted to catch Osama or stop terror or learn a skill or grow up a little or just serve their country, will come home changed, and probably with questions.

They'll want to know why, and how, what happened and what will happen next. They'll want to know about shoddy hospital facilities and slashed benefits, about botched intelligence and torture policies and war profiteering and by the way thank you for the body armor that never arrived.

They'll come home with stories to tell, some of horror and some of humanity persevering in civil war. They might want to know what we thought, and what they missed. They might spend a lot of time with YouTube, catching up.

I have a feeling they might be less concerned with expensive haircuts, hunting histories and who voted for what and when than border security and military readiness, but a few tours in the desert might just lead one to prioritize.

They might take note of the possibility, if not likelihood, that none of the eventual candidates for president in 2008 will have served their country in uniform during a time of war.

And in 10 years or so, maybe less, they'll start cropping up, candidates with "veteran" beside their names, making noise and waves, and somehow that gives me a lot of hope.

Four years ago, I watched representatives of this generation, high-school students at the time, participate in a competition testing their knowledge of the U.S. Constitution. Toward the end, the group was asked how they, as young people, could best keep informed of the actions of their government.

Read newspapers and magazines, I thought. The Internet. C-SPAN.

"Participate in it," they answered, and suddenly I felt old, and dumb, and proud.

I would have spared them this if I could have — terror and war, loss and uncertainty — but other generations have seen it, too, and come back, stronger and with new ideas. So I just do what people have always done, what parents always do: hope, pray, wonder about the future, worry a little, and wait for the kids to come home.

(5/27/08)

Male Neologic

Made-up word for the day: Aerobophobia: (n.) The irrational fear of an elevated heart rate.

On approaching 30, many men will begin working out because they've noticed a couple of extra pounds and maybe a lost step during pick-up basketball games.

On approaching 40, many men will begin working out because of sexual insecurity, a feeling they're losing their appeal.

On approaching 50, many men will begin working out because somebody they know about their age has suddenly dropped dead.

Then there are those of us who begin exercising more because we hope it will decrease the pain we experience on doing strenuous things, such a waking up.

I talked about this the other night with a friend who is my age. "I sit on the edge of the bed for a long time," he said, talking about mornings. Lately I've been doing the same thing. I've been more physically active and my body apparently doesn't think this is healthy, because when I get out of bed I receive numerous neurological messages, most of them (in my opinion) telling me to get back in.

My feet hurt, my joints are stiff, my neck refuses to entertain the concept of a range of motion, and I pray that no one surprises me because I'm pretty sure I can't raise my eyebrows. I only manage to function by sheer will and the mental repetition of what I consider my personal mantra:
Don'twalklikeanoldpersondon'twalklikeanoldpersondon't walklikeanoldperson.

This makes me want to make up more words, such as Sedentation: (n.) A state of being, characterized by increased production of certain neurotransmitters (specifically dopamine and serotonin), usually induced by sitting in a recliner watching television and/or sleeping.

Ambivulatory: (adj.) The inability to decide whether or not one wants to walk.

So I've picked up the pace, which I know sounds counterintuitive but I'm not sure what else I can do. Obviously I could just refuse to move anymore, but that could be problematic (bathroom issues alone trouble me), so I'm making an effort here.

It doesn't help matters that I've been invited to two 30-year reunions in the past year, one high school and the other college. I didn't go; I'm not a masochist. But I saw plenty of pictures of old classmates; "old" as in "former" and "old" as in the distinct impression I got that many of them couldn't make the trip and sent their parents instead.

Hallucinopecia: (n.) The sensation that one has experienced hair loss, but honestly believing it can't possibly be as much as the guy who used to sit next to you in biology class.

I'm not mourning for lost youth here, and I'm still a year or so shy of 50, and 50 is the new 30, of course, which I passionately believe. But I can't deny that some things don't work as well as they used to, including my heart, lungs and most muscles, so becoming proactive seemed like a good idea.

I decided that movement of any kind was an improvement, so I turned my attention to the yard. It's been a few years since I've done much in the way of landscaping other than mowing and some occasional sweeping, so I woke up bright and early one morning and dug a new flower bed.

That was fun. I assume someone else will plant the flowers, since now that sounds like a little too much exertion for me.

Osteopsychosis: (n.) A psychiatric condition in which the patient sincerely believes his or her bones will crumble into dust with any activity more strenuous than thinking.

And in the past week, I've spent an hour every day on the treadmill, which I think is remarkable for a guy whose healthy behavior in the past few years has only consisted of abstaining from alcohol and watching my wife eat vegetables.

The other day, in fact, after 10 minutes or so I had a little (relative) spring in my step, so I cranked up the speed a little (my treadmill has levels, conveniently labeled with terms like "performance," "aerobic" and "fat-burning"; I didn't quite reach those, but at least I was above "why are you bothering?").

Soon the sweat was copious, the endorphins were playing, and my heart rate was 150 and steady. I felt limber, loose, young and energetic, and I saw quite clearly the headline:

"Local Writer Drops Dead On Treadmill; Glasses Still Missing."

Morbidosity: (n.) Oh, look it up.

(5/9/07)

Father's Day

He doesn't care if I write about him, in case you wonder. He rarely reads this column, or anything I write for that matter, and my opinions about him or anything else rarely merit more than an acknowledgment or a bored nod. Everybody's got an opinion.

What he cares about is whether or not there's a Dr. Pepper hidden in the fridge. What he cares about is a ride to the video store. What he cares about is macaroni and cheese the way I make it, the way he likes it, with a rich cheese sauce and store-bought croutons and pasta cooked so al dente it crunches. My boy has priorities.

There was a time when I thought being the father of a little girl was enough for me. Fathers and sons are complicated creatures, Freudian or otherwise, and I wasn't sure I wanted to walk that road. I was on thin ice as it was; maybe it was best not to tempt fate.

We wanted another child, though, or at least that's how I remember the conversation, and soon I was looking at an 8-week ultrasound and knew it was my son, somehow, and I began to imagine what it would be like.

You can get into trouble that way, sometimes.

Five years of living with a precocious daughter prepared me, it turned out, for nothing. Fatherhood, I'd assumed from limited experience, consisted of hugs and only the occasional tantrum, hours spent with alphabet boards and Big Bird, long walks and sunny dispositions, bedtime stories and Disney films.

It did not consist of hiding ladders so I didn't find my 2-year-old son on the roof, trying out this gravity thing. It did not consist of searching madly through a crowded mall for a little boy when our attention was diverted for just one second, finally finding him engaged in unintelligible conversation with nice, if bewildered, shoppers.

It did not consist of confusion, wondering why it took so

106

long for him to speak. It did not consist of other parents, who loved him and smiled when he burst into a room, but had a look in their eyes that I couldn't read. Surely he wasn't the only impulsive kid around. Surely he wasn't the only one who had difficulty playing with others, who seemed strangely inappropriate, who wandered into his own world from time to time and seemed oblivious.

It did not consist of doctors, therapists, psychologists, and neurologists, all trying to answer questions that ultimately came down to: Is there something wrong?

There was something, anyway.

He's a funny guy, usually in a spontaneous, out-of-the-blue way. Towering over me now, 6'3 and 240 pounds, we were walking a while back through a grocery store and, as always, he was bumping into me, walking sideways, unintentionally elbowing me in the aisles.

I got irritated, finally, and called him on it, and he channeled a little Ratso Rizzo, a character from a movie he's never seen but somehow has absorbed, the way he absorbs things he can't explain.

"Hey!" he said, laughing. "I'm AUTISTIC over here!"

We have them for such a short time, we know, just long enough to begin to get a grasp of who they are before they're out the door, off to the future in a hurry, leaving us catching our breath, wondering what exactly just happened.

So I'm fortunate, in that sense. My son will be with me a little longer, his steps a little less sure, a little slower.

I grieved for a boy only once, years ago when I realized what wouldn't happen. I'd never watch him catch a sideline pass, or a foul ball. I'd never slip an extra $20 into his pocket on prom night, help him run for student government, watch him play a solo with the high school orchestra, wait for the sound of a car on a Friday night.

But that was never my boy, and I never could have imagined the joy I get now from this gentle giant who so completely inhabits my world.

It's been four Father's Days now since I had a phone call to make. I meant to write something about my dad this week, about how I miss him and how I still hear him, see him in my dreams and take his counsel.

It turned out, though, that in thinking about fathers I remembered I was one. Still callow in some ways, still learning, still confused and still frustrated, but still needed. And that, as many of you know, is worth celebrating.

Maybe I'll just sit around this Sunday. Or maybe, if the weather goes along, I'll work out in the yard, and maybe my son will join me. He looks after me these days, worries about my bum shoulder and crackling knees, and insists on doing the heavy lifting. I let him, of course, because I have no choice, because I appreciate it, and because I simply enjoy sharing the day with him, and know that at this time of year the sun will be out for hours.

(6/13/07)

Reagan Through Older Eyes

I never voted for him. Part of this came from growing up in a household that suspected Republican politicians, suspected them of shilling for the rich and powerful and ignoring the little guy. Part, I'm sure, came from his tenure as governor of California when we lived in that state; my parents didn't seem to think much of him, and much of the politics of young people can be traced to their parents.

But mostly, I think, it was because I was young and he was old. What millions of Americans found reassuring and solid in Ronald Reagan, I found dated and clichéd. I thought of him as an anecdotal president, more comfortable perpetuating his particular folklore (the welfare queen, the polluting trees) than dealing with issues and substance. I thought of him as shallow, superficial, articulate with a script in front of him and bumbling without.

As I say, I was young, 22 when Reagan defeated Carter in 1980. I was born with the Cold War, came of age and political awareness when detente was the way of the world, peaceful coexistence, and the rhetoric of Ronald Reagan made me nervous, gave me nightmares of nuclear horror.

It surprises me, then, as a lot of things do these days, that the clarity of my vision has changed. I look at what happened 20 years ago and find myself holding history at arm's length, as I now do the label on a medicine bottle, trying to see what used to be so obvious.

Of all the books, the pictures drawn of our 40th president by fans and foes, Peggy Noonan's "What I Saw at the Revolution" gave me a portrait of Ronald Reagan that remains the most vivid. Noonan was a young woman, a passionate conservative and admirer of Reagan, who jumped at the chance to be a junior speechwriter in his White House, and in her book she writes of what she saw through the eyes of a young person, still questioning, still wondering, and watching all the time.

The most powerful man on the planet wrote memos and notes on stationary sent to him by schoolchildren, handmade on cheap paper with an ink stamp. He cheerfully wrote letters on behalf of a couple of elderly women in California, knowing the value of his signature would pay debts that they couldn't.

She writes of a man who spoke eloquently (with Noonan's words) at a memorial for John Kennedy, whom he once (in 1960) compared to Karl Marx. She speaks of a man who was genuinely confused when his political nemesis, Speaker Tip O'Neill, could share jokes and stories with him in the Oval Office and then blast him outside the White House.

And she writes of a man who never wavered in his beliefs and convictions; he'd grown over the years, after all, changing his party affiliation from Democrat to Republican, stumping for Harry Truman in 1948 and Barry Goldwater in 1964. By the time you reach your 70s, he seemed to feel, you know something about the world and how you see it.

There was steel behind the smile, his associates tell us, but mostly we just saw the smile. And maybe it's this, the congeniality and the courtesy and the simple civility of the man, that makes me look back and see him in a different light.

We're still too close for anything but spin; how history will judge the Reagan presidency will be seen by our great-grandchildren. I have no answers, although I did when I was younger, and maybe will again when I'm in my 70s, when I know something of the world and how I see it.

It's just that I find myself wondering more, here in middle-age, seeing shades of gray where once it was crystal-clear black and white, particularly when it comes to history and country and people.

And, as Ms. Noonan pointed out Monday, it was not a shock but still a blow. We knew it would happen one day, we suspected sooner than later, and still here we are, taken back a bit and reflective. I can be as sentimental as the next guy, too.

So I think I will just say this. Following 9/11, both our current president and his predecessor went to New York. Those dark days were perhaps George Bush's finest hour; he reassured America by being strong and decisive.

Bill Clinton walked the streets of Manhattan, comforting stricken citizens, holding a sobbing woman whose husband was still missing and telling her to never to give up hope.

And it struck me, then, that this is what Americans look for in our leaders: someone to lead us, surely, but someone to comfort and reassure us, too, in times of tragedy and terror. And I remember thinking, how rare it is to have a president who can actually do both well.

And, over the past few days, I've been remembering that once, when I was a very young man, we did.

(6/9/04)

Commencement

This is the time of year when, once again, locally famous newspaper columnists like me are inundated with requests to share their wisdom with high school graduates.

Maybe not inundated.

OK, maybe not even asked. But sometimes I don't check my mail.

Anyway, here we are, you about to head out into the real world and me already in the real world, sitting here with all this wisdom. So where do I begin?

At the beginning, of course. Most of you are probably asking yourselves right about now the ultimate question, which is: Where did I come from? Believe me, you should have asked this a long time ago. You have a lot of catching up to do.

I'm here to help, though. As you're probably aware, most of the history of the past fifty-eight years or so has happened since 1946. This is just common knowledge. In 1946, people began having lots of babies, and they kept on doing this until 1964, when they slowed down. This had something to do with The Beatles, I think.

At any rate, all these babies needed a cultural identity. Their parents were, in large part, members of The Greatest Generation, so that name was taken. Instead, they became known as Baby Boomers. They were, among other things, the first television generation and the first generation to make really bad decisions when it came to hairstyles. I am a proud member of this generation.

Babies didn't stop being born, of course, and thus we had a new generation and needed a new name. Gone are the days when generations could go about their business without being called something or other, apparently.

So Generation X was created, sometimes called "the

slacker generation," although that seems a little unfair at this point. We could all be called slackers if we have to compare ourselves to The Greatest Generation.

But, wait. Now it starts to get good. At some point around 1982 or so, it became apparent to demographers, people who notice such things, that a new generation was being born like crazy. This became known in some circles as a baby boomlet, but that never really caught on and so you, proud graduates, are members of Generation Y.

Demographers are not known for their imagination.

But you have a rich cultural history, Generation Y. You could easily be called the first Cable Generation, or VCR Generation, or Computer Generation or Cell Phone Generation. Your childhoods are committed to videotape, which are now being desperately transferred to DVD because your parents are running out of closet space.

You could also be called the File Sharing Generation as we, your doting parents, apparently forgot to mention to you that it was wrong to steal. Our bad. Sorry.

Or we could call you the "X-Files" Generation, I guess, since that TV show came along during the time when you were branching out, seeking your own forms of entertainment apart from your parents' boring, mundane choices like "ER" or The Home Shopping Network.

So here you are, all sort of grown up and graduating and stuff, and you're probably understandably a little nervous. Relax. I'm here to talk you through this. Think of me as your personal Agent Mulder. Or Scully. Whichever was the guy.

What I want to tell you is this: You have lots of time. Remember how it felt to be a freshman, back in the fall of 2000, when the seniors were really tall and threatening and being called "the class of 2004" sounded sort of bizarre and science fiction-y? Now you're freshmen all over again, even if you're pretty tall.

113

You have time to make mistakes. This is a good time for it. Trust me, you don't want to start making mistakes when you're, say, 40. The car insurance alone is horrendous.

Feel free to make a few errors in judgment. Go to college, take a year off, join the service, hitchhike around Europe (don't tell anyone you're an American), get a dumb job and a small apartment, change your major half a dozen times, fall in love, get your heart broken, stay up late and let yourself be lazy once in a while. Life will be waiting for you.

Get enamored of a political candidate or cause and let yourself hope and dream about a better world. Cynicism is hard to unload once it catches hold, and it will.

Understand that the stupidest things you will ever do will be under the influence of drugs or alcohol, so remember moderation, moderation in all things.

Try to hang on to good friends. Come back and visit your favorite teacher; he or she will have an enormous impact on your life, and it's nice to let them know it.

And know that the previous generations, for all our fancy names and numbers, will never again have what you do: A chance to be there at the beginning. It's your turn, class of 2004. So, go already. Be good. Don't steal. Dream a lot.

And turn the damn cell phones off once in a while. I'm just saying.

(6/16/04)

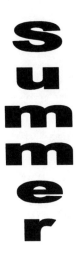

Summer

"In summer, the song sings itself."

--William Carlos Williams

"Summer afternoon - Summer afternoon... the two most beautiful words in the English language."

--Henry James

"We started when we were teenagers, just camping trips then, and next summer the first of us turns 50. The rest will follow soon, maybe reluctantly but inevitably. We are marking time, then, not by grey hairs or aching knees but by a weekend each summer, less reunion than remembering, muscle memory. "

--*My Summer Vacation*, page 132

Survivors

I dream in color, although I guess some folks don't. I don't know what that means, either, if it carries some psychological weight or neurological insight, and honestly for years I couldn't have told you whether I did or not, anyway.

But I do. Because sometimes, now, I dream about an orange pick-up truck and a blue sweatshirt.

The truck belonged to my best friend, Kurt. I can't remember now if it was a Ford or Chevy, or frankly if it was really orange and not burnt sienna or tan or some mixture of rust and brown, but orange is what I see and I can tell you when I saw it last.

Monday, October 13, 1975, I caught my last glimpse of Kurt's truck on the local news, although by then I knew what to expect.

Kurt was ferrying friends home from school, as he did. Steve was riding shotgun. Eric, Kelly and Jeanne were riding in the back. On most days, I'd have been there, too, but I stayed at school for some reason.

It's an old story. A drunk driver. A left turn without yielding, in front of a truck that can't stop fast enough. Five teenagers getting a lesson in physics.

Seatbelts left Kurt and Steve only dazed. Jeanne smashed into the tailgate, breaking her collar bone. Eric flew out of the truck bed and landed, amazingly, on the soft lawn of a nearby house, uninjured.

Eric had the good sense to walk right inside this stranger's house and ask to use the phone. He also had the good sense to call his mother, a block away. Kurt would also find a phone, and call my mother. He gave her the details, choking back tears.

"I think Kelly is dead," he said.

Memories are funny things. What we decide to save, and where. My wedding, for example, is sort of a blur, but I remember odd details about a car accident 28 years ago.

They were my friends. Steve was over at the house all the time. Eric was Kurt's brother. Kelly had been Jeanne's friend since junior high. Jeanne was my sister. So it was personal.

They all survived, surely scarred but alive and resilient, as kids can be. Kelly had brain surgery but she came out of it fine. A couple of weeks later, in fact, I took her to the state fair, and in December we went to the Christmas Formal dance together, and now we get to the blue sweatshirt, finally.

Memories are also funny in the way they sneak up on us, random and cascading and only understood in retrospect.

It's the picture I'm thinking about, of course. I know that now, today, this sunny Sunday so many years away. It was taken on that Christmas Formal night. I stand there, ridiculous sideburns and hair, in my tux. Kurt is wearing a tux, too. And in between us is my father, in that blue sweatshirt. We all look happy, Kurt and I prepared for the big night and Dad just being father to the boys.

He liked Kurt, saw something of himself in this roly-poly kid who smoked cigarettes and was a wizard with tools. And Kurt adopted Dad, found, I think, the father he didn't have. It's a nice picture, and although I don't have it with me I can see it clearly. It's a picture of ghosts.

Kurt died six summers ago, collapsing with a massive heart attack at 41. My father passed away in December 2003 from cancer.

I see them in my dreams, both of them. Kurt is always driving that orange truck, offering me a lift. Dad is usually wearing that blue sweatshirt, always 40, always trying to help me out of some mess involving tools or my house, or else just talking to me.

I'm writing this on Father's Day. My daughter called from Texas, my son gave me a funny gift, and my wife presented me with a dessert so decadent and rich that I was tempted to brush my teeth between bites. And now I sit at the computer, chasing memories from a long time ago.

It's my second June without a call to make or a card to send. It's easier this year. Somehow I wish it wouldn't be easier, but I guess even middle-aged men can be resilient, too.

I heard from Steve a few years ago. My sister just celebrated her 20th wedding anniversary, and in fact a couple of years ago she and her husband spent a nice evening with Eric and his wife at a high school reunion.

And she stays in touch with Kelly, who is, I'm told, still as radiant and lovely as she was at 15, when I took her to a dance, double dating with my friend Kurt.

As I say, memories are funny things, tied to each other and to us in mysterious ways, waiting for an opening. I was just sitting here, thinking about another Sunday, before the accident, when the door opened and Kurt came into my house. He handed my dad a gift, said "Happy Father's Day," and suddenly I'm back there, remembering and smiling and missing them both so much.

(6/22/05)

One For The Books

Do you suppose they knew, 229 summers ago in Philadelphia, what they were doing? In a sense, of course they did; they were tweaking the king and setting themselves up for a dangle at the business end of a rope if things didn't work out.   And they were intelligent, sophisticated guys who knew something about history. Still, I wonder if they envisioned the future, or allowed themselves to imagine a national holiday on the fourth day of July, stretching over the centuries. I wonder what they would have thought of fireworks. Or hot dogs, for that matter.

That's the problem with history. It's hard to know when it's happening.   It'd be nice if it came with some narration so we'd appreciate the moment.

I've seen history, of course. The Berlin Wall coming down. The planes flying into the twin towers. The 2000 Presidential election. But usually it's hard to tell; it takes some time.

It was thinking about this, though, that made me remember one brush with history, eleven years ago, and how I wasn't the only one caught off guard.

It's a baseball story, by the way. So stop reading now if you want.

For the rest of you, it was July 8, 1994. I was home alone, for some reason, watching the Mariners play the Red Sox in Fenway Park. The TV announcer was Skip Carey. I don't know if Skip Carey is still in the broadcast biz, or even if Skip is his real name, but back in 1994 he was pretty young. So maybe we can cut him a little slack.

If you follow Major League Baseball, maybe you remember that season, 1994. If you follow the Mariners, maybe you remember that something started to happen that summer, late July and early August. They started to put some wins together, and suddenly, for the first time in their history, Mariners fans began to sniff October. And then the plug got pulled; an impending players strike caused the owners to cancel the rest of the season, and some people say baseball died then, or at least lost its innocence.

And there are some who say that the sport resurrected itself the following summer, when the Seattle Mariners sprinted out of the All-Star break, caught the Angels, won a tie-breaker game with Anaheim, and beat the Yankees and went to the ALCS on the bat of Edgar Martinez and the legs of Kin Griffey, Jr.

At any rate, on July 8, 1994, in an otherwise uninteresting game, lightning struck. And poor Skip was clueless.

We rely on them, these announcers, if we like the game. We count on them to let us know the score, to feed us details, to keep the narrative moving when we really, really need to go to the refrigerator. They hold down the fort, in other words, let us live and still learn.

Top of the sixth inning. Mariners on first and second. No outs. Marc Newfield at the plate. Both runners moving, a Lou Pinella speciality, a hit and run.

Mike Blowers (on second) takes off with the pitch, as does Keith Mitchell (first). Newfield hits a line drive right at Sox shortstop John Valentin, who takes a step to his left and into the record books.

I really have no business writing about baseball. I'm not a student of the game; I just like to watch. I'm not a baseball historian or an amateur statistician. But I know some things.

Over a century of Major League baseball. Decades of records set and broken, tape measure home runs and no-hitters, strike-outs, perfect games and basket catches, and in all that time what John Valentin did had only been accomplished nine times before. And always in almost exactly the same way.

Even Valentin didn't know. For some reason, he was

120

thinking there was one out already, so he caught the drive, stepped on second to double up Blowers, then sort of nonchalantly tagged the approaching Mitchell for what he supposed was out number four and headed for the dugout.

The rarest of the rare, not just in baseball but all of sports. An unassisted triple play. And do you know what our friend Skippy had to say?

"Umm."

It still makes me smile today. In a matter of seconds, history happened and the announcer was tongue-tied.

OK. No more baseball, I promise. It's just funny, to me, seeing history made. Especially the non-tragedy type. No wars, no attacks, no assassinations. Just a line drive in the right place at the right time.

As I say, we can cut Skip some slack. I wasn't quite sure what I saw, either, and I didn't have a mike in front of me.

Something else happened that night, by the way. Just in case you're still reading.

July 8, 1994, was also the debut of a Mariners rookie by the name of Alex Rodriguez.

Now I'm done. I promise.

And have a great Fourth. Easy on the hot dogs.

(6/29/05)

The Talking Head From Hope

Forgiveness is more art than emotion, more skill than spirituality. It's preached from the pulpit, and a basic tenet of any 12-step program. You have to let go, dump the resentments, let the other guy off the hook and move on. But it's not easy, and it takes practice.

C.S. Lewis once wrote, "If we really want to learn how to forgive, perhaps we should start with something easier than the Gestapo." He was right. I'm not ready to forgive Osama bin laden, for example. And then there was this kid in my sixth-grade class. I'm working on it.

But I forgive Bill Clinton.

There. That wasn't hard at all. Maybe he'll send me a card or something.

It's not a big deal for me, forgiving Bill Clinton. For some of you, you'd rather give the Gestapo a break. I understand this, as much as I can. He rankles you; you see him as a pathological liar, a phony, a philanderer and a bad, bad man, and you've probably seen way more of him in the past week than you're really comfortable with. Hey. I feel your pain.

Clinton with Dan Rather. Clinton with Oprah. Clinton with Larry King (and taking your calls!). Explaining, pontificating, admitting some mistakes, pumping his achievements and pushing his book, our 42nd president has been all over the place lately, reminding us of his intelligence, his flaws, his charm, his disingenuousness, and his apparent inability to ever shut up. The man does like to talk.

His book, "My Life," is on a pace to become the best-selling political memoir of all time, even given the mixed reviews and the fact that we've heard all the good stuff by now. How he slept on the couch for two months. How he had extensive family counseling. How he came to terms with his demons and traced them to a painful home life when he was a kid. How he eats a lot less now.

122

You know. The good stuff.

He remains, statistically, arguably the most popular U.S. president of the past half-century or so, which has many Americans and all of Fox News shaking their collective heads. Few people are neutral about Bill Clinton. He is loved and admired, loathed and hated. And he wasn't even a liberal.

He wasn't, either. He was a pragmatist, which is the nice word for it, or a waffler, which is not so nice. As much as his positions on health care, gays in the military and tax increases outraged the Right, his support of NAFTA and welfare reform irritated the Left. He presided over the greatest peacetime economic expansion in our history, mostly by getting out of the way of it. He was the darling of the Hollywood elite but also of soccer moms, a demographic that won him elections. Women loved Bill Clinton, apparently, and Clinton...well. He liked his cigars.

I'm not trying to be coy, or Clintonesque. I voted for the man twice, eyes wide open. I saw the character questions. I knew what "caused pain in my marriage" meant. I understood that he tried to manipulate the system to stay out of the Vietnam War. I made a choice, is all. I got disappointed a lot, but rarely surprised.

I found and find much to admire about the man: his intelligence, his oratory, his self-described Baby Huey-ness, the inability to be knocked down and beaten back. I thought his impeachment was bogus, an exercise in political frustration, a view many Republicans in Congress (as we know now) shared privately as their arms were twisted very publicly.

But he gave them a sword. He knew the vultures were circling and he still tossed out raw meat. Call it hubris, arrogance, weakness, or, as he does, self-destructive behavior as a result of growing up with an abusive, alcoholic stepfather: It was stupid, and it cost.

I don't need to forgive Bill Clinton for having an affair

with a young woman. That's for his wife and daughter and friends to do. It happens. None of us are immune to temptation, whether it's Clinton's adultery or George W. Bush drinking himself stupid for years before he cleaned up. Show me a perfect president, or human being.

And Kennedy's sexual adventures and Nixon's lies make Bill Clinton look like an amateur, just to name two.

What I have to forgive is Clinton being dumb on my nickel and my vote, for dragging all of us into his personal life and putting the country on hold for months while the circus came to town. There's plenty of blame to spread around, but he's responsible and, as he liked to say, he was working for us. We are guilty of lots of civic faults, you and I, but we deserved better.

So I forgive him, even if Al Gore and Monica maybe can't. I'm moving on. Life's too short to hold a grudge. I'm over it.

But Bill. Dude. Stop and take a breath once in a while, OK? It's exhausting me.

(6/30/04)

124

Trivial Pursuit

There's been a rumor floating around certain journalists on the Internet for a few months now, and finally a story has broken, in The New Republic. According to the authors, they've been told by sources within Pakistani intelligence that a lot of pressure is being put on them (Pakistan) by certain American movers and shakers, including a White House aide, to try really, really hard to capture some big name al Qaeda operatives this summer, up to and including Osama himself. They've even been given some dates to try really, really hard; namely, the last 10 days of July in general, and around July 26 in particular.

Those of you who pay attention and follow events closely understand, of course, the significance of July 26. It is, as you know, my birthday.

I am truly honored.

July 26 also happens to be the start of the Democratic Convention in Boston, which makes the story interesting, if probably impossible to prove. If you choose to believe it, it raises questions, chief among them: Wouldn't it make more sense to try really, really hard to capture the bad guys on somebody else's birthday? How about Frank Lloyd Wright's? I'm just suggesting.

What it does show us, though, is that things are heating up in the silly season. Talking points have been Fed X-ed and the spin is all around. Kerry flip-flops on issues. Bush is sending jobs overseas. Kerry is a decorated Vietnam vet who fights for his country. Bush stood up to the terrorists and fights for his country. The economy is in recovery. The economy is in mild recovery. The economy is in a fake recovery.

And veepmanship plays a part, too. John Edwards is the son of a mill worker who became a TRIAL LAWYER and worked his way through college so he could be a TRIAL LAWYER and is a smooth-talkin' Southerner who is also a TRIAL LAWYER and he has a sunny disposition because he got rich being a TRIAL LAWYER. Meanwhile, Dick Cheney gives colorful advice to Sen. Patrick Leahy.

There've been distortions on both sides; nothing new here. And there'll be talk of bounces and setbacks and October Surprises and voting machines. It's a tight race, with Mr. Bush slipping beneath 50% approval (a dicey thing, historically, for an incumbent) but Mr. Kerry not exactly lighting fires. Yawn.

So, in looking for anything possibly interesting in all this, I noticed something. John Kerry and John Edwards both are married to women older than them.

So am I. It's an admirable trait, then.

It did make me wonder, though. So I did a little checking. Just for fun.

Five presidents married older women. George Washington, Millard Fillmore, Benjamin Harrison, Warren Harding, and Richard Nixon.

James Buchanan never married, the only one.

Grover Cleveland married a woman nearly 30 years younger (the longest age span among presidential couples), and was the only president to be wed in the White House. His daughter, Esther, was the only child to be born in the White House.

Harding was the first president to speak on the radio, the first to visit Alaska (and Canada), and the first to have his father outlive him. He also had the largest feet of any president (size 14).

Lincoln, at 6'4, was the tallest. James Madison was the smallest, 5'4 and less than 100 lb.

Gerald Ford was actually born Leslie Lynch King, Jr. (President King sounds funny, doesn't it?) and is the only president to have been an Eagle Scout.

Ronald Reagan was not only the oldest elected president, but lived longer than any other (93), although Mr. Ford is gaining.

Washington refused to shake hands, believing it was

beneath a president; he bowed.

John Adams was the great-great-grandson of John and Priscilla Alden. His last words were, "Thomas Jefferson survives," although this was not true; Jefferson succumbed a few hours before, both of them dying on July Fourth, 1826, fifty years after the Declaration was signed.

James Monroe also died on Independence Day.

Jefferson wrote own epitaph, by the way, and didn't mention that he'd been president.

John Q. Adams swam nude in the Potomac River every morning at 5 a.m., prompting Jane Royall, the first professional journalist, to come and sit on his clothes until he agreed to be interviewed, thus landing the first presidential, um, sit-down.

Ten religious affiliations are associated with our presidents, with Episcopalians leading the pack (11) and Presbyterians following (7). Four presidents had no religious affiliation at all, including Lincoln.

Nearly half (21) of our presidents were born in the 19th century, although only one on July Fourth (Calvin Coolidge) and none, as it turns out, on July 26, which makes this whole exercise sort of trivial.

But it beats listening to speeches and spinners, if you ask me. Besides, somehow I find it comforting to know that we have a colorful presidential history to peruse, that they were all human with flaws and virtues and quirks, and that some of them, like me, Edwards and Kerry, were married to older women, among them Warren G. Harding, who also had really, really big feet.

Me, I wear size 10-1/2, but that's probably more than you wanted to know.

(7/14/04)

The Sweet Swing of Success

If you're as obsessive as the rest of America, or me, you now know who Ken Jennings is.

The thirty-something from Salt Lake City, who looks like a cross between a generic CNN reporter and the long-lost brother on "Fraser," ran the table on "Jeopardy!" in the past month or so, accumulating over a million dollars by answering, roughly, every question. Until the show went on hiatus for the rest of the summer, during which time I suspect they will be busy changing the rules and/or pouring maple syrup into his buzzer thingy. No one likes a smarty-pants.

I have a question, now, for Ken, and you, in the category of "Sports Sayings." It's this: "He wrote, 'It's not whether you win or lose, but how you play the game.'"

No fair using the Internet.

Ha! I win.

Because it was a trick question. I did it on purpose.

Although undoubtedly many people have used that particular phrase, what they are misquoting is a line from the pen of Grantland Rice. "When the One Great Scorer comes to write against your name/He marks- not that you won or lost - but how you played the game."

Rice was a truly Modern Man, born during the American Industrial Revolution and living into the Atomic Age, but he also was a prototype, leading the way for Bob Costas and Howard Cosell (not in that order). He was the first superstar sports journalist, elevating the games people play by (mostly) purplish prose and a fan's devotion. If you ever find yourself using football, say, as a metaphor for life (and please don't), you owe a debt to Grantland Rice, because he invented the idea.

Rice's most famous writing is about the "Four Horsemen," a column referring to the 1925 Notre Dame backfield, but he was also responsible for legends that live on, particularly Jim Thorpe and Bobby Jones.

I'm writing today about Bobby Jones. Sort of.

Bobby Jones in the Twenties was to golf what today Tiger Woods is to...well, golf. He had the same preternatural ability, but without the bucks, and he may (Tiger still working) have been the greatest golfer of all time.

I know next to nothing about golf, actually. I watch it on TV when I feel the urge to take a nap. I tolerate my wife's passion for this game, a little ball and a little stick. Come on. We've got BASEBALL.

But I can admire it, admire the skill and the precision, and admire the ones who do it best.

I played golf once, only once, 22 years ago, early in the morning, nine holes on a public course in Phoenix, Arizona, with my dad and Allen O'Reilly. My dad was 45, and Allen and I were in our early twenties. None of us resembled Bobby Jones, or Tiger. But it was early.

Dad eventually gave up golf. Me too. I don't know about Allen. But he was my friend, a college roommate who passionately wanted to be a good actor. He eventually left school and moved to Atlanta, where he married a lovely woman from the Carolinas and fathered a couple of boys, and now is in his sixteenth year at the Georgia Shakespeare Festival, currently the Education Director.

John Kennedy once said that mothers across America want their children to grow up to be President, but not politicians. This is true of actors, too. You might not complain if your son-in-law is Tom Hanks, but if he's scrabbling along the streets of Manhattan, looking for work, I can see where you might have questions. So the actor who perseveres requires respect, at least from me.

I haven't seen Al in nearly 20 years, although we stay in touch through Christmas cards and email. But wasn't I writing about Bobby Jones?

Bobby Jones died in 1971, nearly completing his three

score and ten but living the majority of it in pain from a degenerative illness. He found the time after his retirement at 28, though, to found the Masters Tournament at Augusta. And last year, a movie was finally made about his life. "Bobby Jones: Stroke of Genius" may have slipped under your radar. It was released in March and is coming to a video store near you, probably soon.

I'm going to buy the DVD. Not because I care about golf, but because I love stories of talent and perseverance. It stars Jim Caveizel ("The Passion of the Christ") as Jones, but that's not the attraction. It's because, in this film, the small but pivotal role of Grantland Rice is played by my friend Allen O'Reilly.

So much of life is timing. There are smarter people than Ken Jennings who never make the cut on "Jeopardy!" There are certainly better actors than Tom Hanks who never get their break. When I heard from Allen the other day, it reminded me of all of this. Chance, and luck, and devotion to dreams. We'd talk, twenty-plus years ago, he and I, of the future and what might happen. Life is funny, of course, and there are roads not taken and courses not played, but it was sure nice to find out that sometimes wishes come true.

(7/28/04)

A Matter of Degrees

In 1929, a Hungarian writer, whose name you don't know and won't find in this column because my spellchecker software gets too upset, suggested in a short story an intriguing theory about people and connections.

In brief, this theory states that any two people on the planet can find a connection through no more than five other people. Chuck knows Dave, Dave works with Eileen, Eileen knows Pierre, Pierre met Olga at a conference, and Olga's sister married Vladimir, although it didn't work out. Chuck to Vladimir. Six steps.

It became known as Six Degrees of Separation, after an American sociologist in 1967 decided to test the theory. He called it "the small-world problem," and his results surprised a lot of people. He gave random people in the Midwest packages that were to be sent to a man in Massachusetts. They knew the man's name and occupation, and had a general idea of where he was located. They were instructed to give the package to a friend or acquaintance they felt had the best chance of knowing someone who knew someone, etc. They figured it would take hundreds of people.

Actually, the average was between 5 and 7. So they were a little off.

I have no idea what was in the package, by the way. Maybe a fruitcake.

This was a small experiment, but with the advent of faster computers and the Internet, it's been repeated many times since then with similar results, including what became a popular party game, Six Degrees of Kevin Bacon (try to connect the actor with another actor in six steps, mostly by using the Internet Movie Database). And scientists have found practical uses, particularly in disease transmission and corporate communication. We seem to be closer than we might think.

I have my own example of Six Degrees, although I can do it in four and there's not much in the way of science behind it, just history. Still, it fascinates me.

When Abraham Lincoln was born in February 1809, Thomas Jefferson was president, if briefly. A month later, James Madison was sworn in (inaugurations were held in March back then). So the author of the Declaration of Independence and the Father of the Constitution, our third and fourth presidents, respectively, were still alive and serving the new republic when our 16th was born.

When Lincoln was assassinated in 1865, his body was borne from Washington, D.C. to Illinois through various cities, and in New York, from an apartment window, 6-year-old Theodore Roosevelt watched the procession.

In 1912, when T.R. was running for president on the Bull Moose (Progressive) ticket, he shook the hand of a small boy.

And when that small boy retired from a life of teaching high school mathematics, he shook mine.

Four jumps from 1975 to the Founders.

Let's do the math. Lincoln was 57 when he died. Roosevelt was 54 when he shook my teacher's hand. My teacher was in his mid to late sixties when he retired.

Call it my Theory of Grandparents, then. Feel free to use it. Just say, "theory by Chuck," or something. That's fine.

In other words, if you want to connect to history, if you want to learn what it was like, if you want to hear some great stories, you probably need to skip a generation.

My parents had three kids between the ages of 19 and 23. I became a father at 26, and then again at 31. These gaps can vary widely, of course (see: Larry King), but if we just eyeball average a number, looking around, a 30-year age difference between parents and children seems reasonable to play with here.

Thirty years is not long enough. The cultural

differences are there but subtle. The technological ones are more striking, but sort of a done deal to the next generation. You can only talk about rotary dial phones and only four TV channels before their eyes glaze over.

So it's the grandparent generation that provides the insight, the look into a world no longer with us and the history we didn't know.

And, unfortunately, we're usually too young to appreciate it until they're gone.

So I will hold my stories of the wonders of color television and the turmoil of the 1960s for the next generation, when and if they appear. And I find myself drawn to people older than I, wanting to ask questions. What was it like? What did you wear? How did you think? Sometimes I ask; I should ask more. You should, too. We're a young nation, and much of our history resides in the memories of those still with us.

One final example, then. In 1958, the year I was born, the space race was just beginning. The Cold War was heating up. Elvis was in the Army, Ike was in the White House, Castro was heading for Havana, a majority of Americans owned a television set, and we had thermonuclear weapons capable of riding on intercontinental ballistic missiles for thousands of miles. It was a modern world.

And in March of 1958, four months before I was born, John Salley died at the age of 112, the last veteran of the Civil War.

I sure hope someone was asking him questions.

(8/17/05)

My Summer Vacation

There is no mission, and there never was. There are no rapids to shoot, no trout to catch, no mountains to climb. No animals will be harmed during this production. It just is what it is.

We started when we were teenagers, just camping trips then, and next summer the first of us turns 50. The rest will follow soon, maybe reluctantly but inevitably. We are marking time, then, not by grey hairs or aching knees but by a weekend each summer, less reunion than remembering, muscle memory.

Fragments of jokes or movie lines result in spontaneous combustion, laughs or smiles. We know where we've been and what we've done, whom we've known and why we are who we are, for better or worse, and we know it naturally, organically, automatically. That's what 30-plus years will get you. Familiarity like this becomes more than second nature; it's like knowing what side of the bed you sleep on. Some things just are because they always have been.

There were four of us in the beginning, in the mid-1970s, and sometimes there still are, although Randy tends to go AWOL. He's an itinerant engineer, footless in his 40s now, no wife at the moment and no kids, so he tends to wander. Last I heard he was in Georgia, but one of these days he'll call or e-mail and ask, "Do you guys still go away for a weekend in the summer?" and I'll say yes and he'll say, "Damn! Next year I'll be there" and maybe he will.

The other three of us, though, hang on to tradition, even if the geography changes from time to time. Last year we hiked Crater Lake. This past week we went to Whidbey Island.

Maybe it's something about three middle-aged men traveling alone, no wives, no kids, no briefcases, but nearly every year there's a waitress story, and usually it involves an insult, unintentional or not. This time, we walked into a restaurant Saturday and the first words out of the waitress's mouth were, "I can't serve you alcohol."

It was 9 o'clock in the morning.

Now, in fairness to this young woman, she went on to explain that the night bartender had accidentally gone home with the keys to the liquor cabinet in his pocket. And I noticed that at the very top of the menu they offered Bloody Marys and mimosas. Still, we couldn't help wondering if there was something about us that looked like trouble. And we got another story.

We pretty much covered the island, from Langley to Deception Pass. We walked through a winery, played with a dog, sat on the beach, wandered through Coupeville, and took lots of pictures. John Stone, the owner of Captain Whidbey Inn, took us out on his 52-foot sailboat for a two-hour tour of Penn Cove, a ride we shared with a woman from Minnesota. She was good company, curious and bubbly, and over the afternoon we got to know each other.

She was fascinated by the fact that my friend, David, not only shares his life with a woman who is a professional puppeteer, but he writes books about movies. After a long discussion, she said, "OK, so I know what you do," and turning to me she asked, "How about you?" I pointed at David.

"I write about him," I said, and in a way that's true.

Every year I try to make sense of it, explain it, diagram it in a way others can understand, and I don't think I can, really. "But what do you guys DO?" people will ask, and the answer is whatever we feel like, and sometimes not much at all. We laugh. We talk. We catch up. We hang out for a weekend, the way we did when we were kids and none of us could imagine families and mortgages.

Sometimes, as this year, it's the only summer vacation any of us gets, but rather than trying to cram a week into two days, we mostly just take a breath. We're different, anyway; given our preferences, Bill would see everything and do everything, Dave would wander through every bookstore in town, and I'd just sit and look at the water. So we do a little of everything, and it's still hard to explain.

It's becoming more sedate. I noticed two pieces of pizza went uneaten and several bottles of beer went home with Dave, something inconceivable a few years ago. Nobody stays up past midnight anymore, and by 6:30 or so we're up and looking at the day. We all bring dental floss. We're considerate about not using too much hot water when we take our showers. And hey: We take showers.

On Sunday, we policed the cottage we'd rented, wiping crumbs off the table and neatly stacking the pizza boxes. We double- and triple-checked to make sure no one left anything behind (cell phone chargers can be casualties). And we crossed off another weekend with the guys.

Dave and I sat on the back deck one more time, looking over the lagoon. "I think this was the best one," he said, and it occurred to me that we probably say that every year, which is probably why we keep doing it, and probably why we should.

(08/24/05)

Away From Home

You'll never guess where I am.

I'll give you a hint. Travel in a south-easterly direction sixty miles or so from Dallas, Texas, into Kaufman County, and if you pay attention you will eventually end up in Gun Barrel City.

Gun Barrel City is the greatest name for a Texas town there ever was. If Gun Barrel City didn't exist, someone would have had to invent it. Gun Barrel City sounds like a combination of a John Ford movie, a dime novel, and a cheesy Rodgers and Hammerstein musical with a show stopper called, "Smile When You Say That, Stranger."

I can tell you some things about Gun Barrel City. It used to be a small town until it got a Wal-Mart. Now it's a small town with a Wal-Mart. I can tell you where the WhatABurger is. If you've never lived in or visited Texas, New Mexico or Arizona, you don't understand WhatABurger. WhatABurger is a good reason to go to Texas, and sometimes I need a good reason.

But I'm not in Gun Barrel City.

If you head southwest from Gun Barrel City, you'll eventually pick up I-35 South, which will take you through Lyndon Johnson territory. I-35 will take you past Waco, Temple, lots of little towns, the state capitol of Austin, San Marcos, approximately 50 WhatABurgers (I stopped counting), and eventually into San Antonio, where you will find yourself on a Saturday night having Mexican food with a couple of old friends you've just met.

That is, if you're me.

This was Gordon and Michael, who are, respectively, a Baptist minister and a radio news anchor. Gordon is the minister of a small church in north San Antonio. Michael is Gordon's good friend, but also a deacon in this very same church. I have exchanged ideas, thoughts, philosophy, dreams, and concerns with these guys for a while now; in Gordon's case, about a year and a half.

I just never got around to actually meeting them until Saturday.

This is the Good Side of the Internet, the side that dismisses spam and porn and creates friendships based on old-fashioned reasons: Things in common. We've come to know each other, know about the families that enrich our lives and the goals that elude us, the little successes and the disappointments. I know these guys. And now I know what they look like.

I had to have Mexican food. Everyone said so. Michael and Gordon insisted. I tried to explain that I grew up in Arizona, that I understood about regional differences but still I knew what an enchilada was, but they were adamant. And they were right. It was excellent food, and excellent conversation.

It was such an odd experience, hanging out in a strange town with strangers, but they weren't, really. They were friends, good friends, interesting friends, and I had a great time.

But I'm not in San Antonio.

My daughter and I flew into Dallas via Denver on Friday afternoon, traveling from DFW to Arlington to pick up a car we'd helped her buy on the (of course) Internet, driving from there to Gun Barrel City to see her grandparents and allow me to test drive this new car on the road to San Antonio. I drove back to Gun Barrel on Sunday afternoon, stopping for my second WhatABurger, and this morning we packed that car and drove two hours to Denton, home of the University of Texas, where she starts her second year.

So that's where I am, typing this on a desk in a dorm room, aware of an anxious editor in Mukilteo, having spent the day moving furniture and unrolling carpets, sweating like crazy and starting to think that 98% humidity isn't all it's cracked up to be.

See, she's staying this time. She's a music major, meaning she looks forward to an uncertain life, and she figures she might as well start working on the uncertainty now. She's already a second-semester sophomore, and her plan is to attend summer school and start her third year already a senior. Then there is the question of a job, an eventual apartment, all the accoutrements of an adult life that's just starting.

So Dad came along, to help, to bring out his wallet from time to time, to look over the car and unpack boxes, and to see her off. Dads do that.

Tonight, after more shopping for stuff and dinner and meeting some of her friends, I head for the house of my wife's aunt, a wonderful woman who will offer me a room for the night and then drive me to the airport tomorrow for the trip home. I look forward to it, really. Give me some rain, please, and my own bed.

All the way home, of course, I'll have my usual anxiety. I'll keep patting my pocket to ensure that I didn't forget my wallet. I'll check my one carry-on bag to make sure I have everything. I'll worry still, as I always do on a trip, that being slightly muddle-brained as I am I may have left something behind in Texas.

And it'll probably be a week or two before it finally sinks in that I did, and what it was.

(8/25/04)

Off the Map

There's a place just out of eyesight that I think about sometimes. I know it's there, like I know the light in the refrigerator goes off when I close the door, but I don't actually see it.

Sometimes I get philosophical and call it Hope. Or The Future. Sometimes I get depressed and think of it as The Road Not Taken. And sometimes I get faintly sacrilegious and call it Godland.

I've been there. I've lived there for long periods, secure in my serenity. Other times, it's been just a concept, something I believe in but can't wrap my brain around at the moment. It's a place of spiritual sustenance, in other words, and life being as complicated as it is I sometimes lose track of it. I stare out a window and the blinds are closed. It happens. We can get sort of disconnected.

So I'm always glad to find a reminder, and the other night it came, as sometimes it does, in words and pictures and performance. A movie, I mean.

"New Mexico is a very powerful place."

Campbell Scott is the 45-year-old son of George C. Scott and Colleen Dewhurst, a gene pool that sends shivers down my spine. He's done a fair amount of acting, and a little directing, and a couple of years ago he took a play and turned it into a film that not enough people will see, I think.

"Off the Map" is about Charley, Arlene, George, William, and Bo, although sometimes she calls herself Cecilia Rose. Bo is 11, and she has big plans, most of which center around leaving home.

Home is northern New Mexico, in the middle of nowhere, off the map. Somehow, for some reason, Charley, a Korean War veteran, and Arlene, half-Hopi, leave the modern world and make their own rules. They own their house, what it is, no plumbing or electricity, grow their

140

own food, find all sorts of stuff at the dump, and manage. George, Charley's best friend, stops by a lot, is a member of the family, although he has a real job and some real dreams.

One day William, currently an IRS auditor but formerly a short-order cook with a law degree, stops by to discover why this family hasn't filed a tax return in seven years. Arlene explains that they used to, but since they make less than $5000 a year they just thought it unnecessary after a while.

"They still like you to file," William says, sort of ruefully, and then he gets sick and stays on their couch and eventually he just stays.

I can't tell you how much this film moved me, or really even why. Part of it is memory, being a child, driving through the desert with my family from Phoenix to California on trips, wondering what was off the highway, imagining taking a right turn down that dirt road and going on to something else.

Part of it is my self-sufficient side, the side of me that has always said, "Leave me alone and I'll figure it out," the part that wants to be free of instructions and demands, and marvels at a story of people who actually do that.

Part of it is New Mexico; the true Southwest, I thought on my first visit. Phoenix was processed culture but New Mexico was real, and this movie, among all its other charms, has some stunning scenery.

Part of it is that the characters are all basically good and decent people, with no agendas, just staying alive and reading Melville aloud by kerosene light, saying prayers over the animals they kill for food and drinking water by the pitcher, because water is good and it's hot outside.

And part of it is that Charley is sad, this summer, the summer of 1974, the summer the movie covers. Catatonic sad, sometimes. He barely speaks and he stares at nothing, and those around him do a dance, keep moving in hopes that he'll catch the rhythm again, raise the blinds, find his Godland.

The film has its own pace, so be prepared. No shooting or helicopter crashes. No sex. No mysteries, except the ones we all deal with daily. And maybe you won't like it. Maybe it will bore you, if this sort of character study, small story, isn't what you look for in a movie.

I have no business reviewing movies anyway, not here, not anywhere. I don't watch enough of them, or have the background to write an intelligent critique.

But sometimes I find a gem, and it's hard not to mention. Last week, my wife and I both got some spiritual sustenance from a story. And there's joy here, and sweetness, and a couple of surprises, and a sailboat.

And watercolors. But that's all I'm saying.

So rent "Off the Map," if you're in the mood for a movie. It stars Joan Allen and Sam Elliott. It didn't make a lot of money. It was a quiet film, a reminder, maybe, is all. That there's beauty in family. There are powerful places. The sky touches the earth in surprising ways. And open the blinds, from time to time, and look.

(8/31/05)

The Day After

We know where we were and even what we were doing, and for most of us on this side of the country I suspect we were doing the same sorts of things. Waking up, eating breakfast, drinking coffee, sitting in traffic. The day was just beginning, after all, for us.

As I recall, September 11, 2001, was Aaron Brown's first day as a CNN anchor. I could be wrong, but he was the new guy at any rate, and it was reassuring to see him. He was a familiar face, a local face, and I needed to see something familiar if only to balance the strangeness and horror of watching the towers crumble and smoke pour through Manhattan.

And at the end of that long, hard day, Aaron and company speculated aloud on what would happen next. The death toll was to remain a mystery, although it eventually was much lower than we feared. The economic costs couldn't be calculated, not then, but we knew they'd be there. We also knew that retaliation would come, probably sooner than later, but that was still a question, that day.

Mostly they told us that we would be different, that we would be changed forever by what happened on Sept. 11. And I wondered about that, how this change would manifest, whether it would be subtle or huge or somewhere in the middle, and I'm still not sure. Aside from the ripples of loss that affect so many of us, either from the initial attack or the military action in the last four years, and some inconvenience while traveling, I'm not sure we've changed all that much. And I'm not sure but that I think this is a good thing, a resilient thing, a refusal to bow to terror.

But I think we're changed now, after the last week.

Comparing an act of terror and an act of God is a dicey thing, one event perpetrated by evil and the other by warm waters and the vagaries of nature. Still, we watch

143

and we listen and we read and we know this one is worse. Far worse.

We have lost an iconic city, maybe for months, maybe for years. Maybe forever. The emotions we all felt following 9/11 are there, too: horror, grief, anger, resolve. But I've noticed, as I assume you have, something else, something powerful.

America is outraged.

It crosses political lines, class lines and race lines. We watched the poorest of Americans, in a city where 25% of the population falls below poverty levels and 50% of the children do, die in the heat, on the street, waiting for help that took too long to come. Babies died of dehydration. Elderly people died for lack of medication. Others died at the hands of the thugs who crawl out from beneath their rocks whenever given a chance. Meanwhile, federal officials went on television, congratulated themselves and lied to us.

You can hear the outrage in the street, read it in the paper, see it in the faces of reporters. It's not supposed to happen here, not like this, not abandonment to anarchy and death for days. And the outrage is tinged with fear, for the overwhelming message we get from Katrina is this: Four years after 9/11, after the Department of Homeland Security, we are not ready. And next time it could be us.

I disagree with those who say this is not the time for blame, as if we were a nation of unitaskers, capable of either giving help or pointing fingers but not both, or more. But blame is not enough, even if there's plenty to go around, local and federal. What we need are questions being asked, and being asked yesterday. And perhaps those of us in this area feel it more acutely. While the governor of Louisiana declared a state of emergency three days before Katrina hit (a fact that has been obscured and lied about repeatedly in the past days; shame), Gov. Gregoire or those who follow her will have no such opportunity when a 9-plus earthquake strikes. So it's all about the day after.

There is hope amidst the helplessness and the incompetence, though, and along with the stories of horror and despair we'll get other stories. Stories of sacrifice and courage. Stories like the one of the three college sophomores from Duke University who drove to New Orleans, posed as journalists, crammed one sick man and three women in the backseat and drove them to Baton Rouge, dropping the man at a hospital and the women at homes of relatives after buying them dinner. Then they went back and got three more.

Still, we will be changed by what we saw, the misery and the suffering, the apparent incompetence of bureaucrats, the delays and the death. We will want answers, and accountability. We will want to know how the system will be fixed for next time, knowing there will be a next time. And yes, we will open our wallets and our hearts, and for some of us our houses, because that's what we do best in this country.

And we will remember, and rebuild, hope and pray, give and give more, and maybe some of us will listen to a little more jazz, the American invention, the gift of the Crescent City. Just to be reminded that sweetness and sorrow often walk hand in hand, and that the sound of a saxophone never hurt anybody, not ever.

(9/7/05)

Stardust Memories

Stare at the stars long enough, and you'll begin to see things that aren't there.

"Look," I'd tell my kids, years ago. "You're seeing a sky that isn't there anymore, and hasn't been for millions or billions of years." Light races at the legal limit to brighten our nights here, I told them, so far away from home. They'd wonder about that then, try to wrap their brains around the idea, the notion of looking up and backward at the same time.

I can't tell them anything anymore. They've either heard it, know it, think they do, or want to learn all by themselves. I've lost my audience, then. It happens.

I don't need to crane my neck to peruse the past, of course. I just have to look around, sit on my front deck and travel in time.

From the second grade to the eighth, I completed a school year in the same place only once. We moved a lot, so the idea that I've lived in this house for 16 years stuns me sometimes. And particularly what I've lived through.

Of my four closest neighbors, all of them couples, past their child-rearing age when we moved in, three remain, still pretty much the same. We wave and talk as we always have, mailbox meetings. They never mention the weeds I haven't pulled. They ask how the kids are doing. Maybe young parents with small children were a reminder for them, back then, a novelty. They looked after my kids, at any rate, kept an eye out and visited with them and bought stuff they had to sell.

Listen: This is what I can see from my porch. I can see a 3-year-old girl, racing across the front lawn and back again, pretending to be a Princess of Power. I can see a 5-year-old towhead boy, wandering from house to house, carrying on a nonstop conversation with neighbors who probably catch every tenth word.

These are nice ghosts for me, shadows with training

wheels and loud voices, jumping from the swing at its apex and rolling in the grass, laughing. I sit and watch them all over again, seeing what isn't there anymore.

There are more corporeal remnants of 16 years. Lots of bikes, lots of videos, lots of books, only laziness and sentiment preventing a good garage sale.

My son went to high school the other day, leaving the only house he's ever lived in, the house we brought him home to from the hospital. I dropped him off in front and watched him walk inside, and for a moment panic grabbed onto my heart and squeezed. I was just seeing a ghost, though. He's two inches taller than I am and he can find his way around now, although I can still see him at 3, remember the Velcro strap I'd wrap around his wrist and mine to keep us from getting separated at school carnivals or the mall.

The strap might be in the garage, too.

I can see me, too. I was two weeks past my 20s when we moved in, and I'd sit on the deck and wonder about responsibility and what would come, imagining and seeing things that hadn't happened yet.

And now here I am.

It's quiet at night. I can smell the grass and the water. I can hear things, and if I'm patient, and stick around, I'll notice the faint laughter of a child, and realize that I can also see the future from the front deck.

Our light will bounce around, too, travel somewhere else, always alive someplace. I will be long gone and my deck will be dust, but the light from this planet will be racing along into the future at 186,000 miles a second, along with TV signals and talk shows. And maybe certain frequencies, in the range of a child's voice, can pierce the atmosphere and go on. There was certainly a lot of that here, once.

But it's not a ghost I hear, not this time.

A young family moved next door a couple of years ago, with a baby.

He's a little boy now, two years old or so. I listen to him, listen to his little boy sounds, the shrieks and the protests and the laughter. So we've come full circle, and here I am, the neighbor with no little children.

He doesn't wander yet; he's still cautious, still watched, still guarded carefully. There's a busy street, and other things.

But maybe one day, maybe in a few years, his parents will relax a bit, knowing they're surrounded by watchers and neighbors, and he will get a little brave and walk over to my front yard and see me, sitting on the porch, staring at the stars.

And if he's really brave, he'll ask me.

"What are you looking at?"

And I'll tell him, then, and maybe he'll try to wrap his brain around the idea. Maybe I'll tell him about how long I've lived in this house. Maybe I'll tell him about when I had a little boy, and a little girl. Or maybe I'll just sit quietly and watch the sky with him, hoping he'll understand that, on a clear night, you can see pretty much everything from here.

(9/8/04)

30 Years in Casablanca

A few weeks ago, my friend Dave and I headed south for the eighth time in as many years.

Eight Saturday mornings, bags packed, sleepy but smiling in anticipation of a weekend with the guys only. We've taken turns driving, heading for Oregon, starting off slow and then waking up and talking nonstop along the way. Thirty years is a long time to be friends and still in your 40s, still hanging on to stories. There are no blank spots in our friendship, no missing years. We remember 15 as well as 45, sometimes better. We graduated high school together the same night from the same school, we both got married in the same year, and we both ended up in Washington State, 1200 miles from home and glad to be here.

I can still see him, walking down the street on the way to my house, 30 years ago this summer, me standing at the doorway and telling him to hurry, Nixon had left and Gerald Ford was about to be sworn in. That's how long it is.

Our transportation in the beginning was bikes, then junky cars that leaked oil a quart at a time. We've lived through parents' homes and small apartments and finally houses of our own. We've shared birthdays and weddings and deaths and (mostly exaggerated) stories of girlfriends.

We've been neighbors at times, and separated by lots of miles at others.

Dave got out of night school one evening in late 1980, turned on the radio and heard the words, "John Lennon is dead," and I came over and we had a wake, him and me, listening to music and wondering about the harshness of it all.

We walked to high school in the beginning, in Phoenix, and then one early morning in the late 1980s we stood together, as we usually did, at a bus stop on Capitol Hill in Seattle, on our way to work, and thought about the oddity of that.

One Saturday in our late 20s, we decided to rediscover our youth and took a basketball to a nearby elementary school. We shot around for about 40 minutes, huffing and puffing, and finally one of us made a basket and then we went and had a beer.

Over the years, we have seen hundreds of movies together and shared enough pizza and potato chips to give us sympathy for Bill Clinton's arteries.

And now, the fall of 2004, we share something else.

Within a month or two of each other, Dave and I will have books published.

Can you imagine? Could we have?

Mine is nothing, a collection of columns and essays.

His comes from a particular passion for odd things, eclectic things, in this case a love of European spy films of the 1960s. It's called "The Eurospy Guide," published by Midnight Marquee Press and available at Amazon.com, I would imagine, by the time you read this column. It's a reference book, essentially, a guide to a particular genre of cinema that intrigued him, so he wrote about it.

There's an inertia about friendship, definable but still mysterious. There are great forces to thwart it, distance and time, maybe one final argument where things are said that can't be taken back, families and responsibilities, and interests that create gaps that even a long history can't fill. A guy who likes to golf is probably going to lose interest in a childhood friend who spends his Saturdays working with wood, for example.

So I have no explanation for why I'm still friends with this guy. Maybe it's just the proximity. Maybe it's just that we haven't run across an irresistible force yet to call a halt to friendship.

It's not a lifestyle thing. He's never had kids, or wanted them. He lives in the city, and I live in the suburbs. The man has no lawn to mow. I mean, really. What do we

150

talk about?

It's not European spy flicks with subtitles and cheesy plots, I know that.

What we have, I guess, is 30 years. Thirty years of supporting, encouraging, taunting, chastising, enlightening and laughing a lot. And now he's an author, and I think, damn. I'm proud of you, man.

We headed to Klamath Falls in early August, and we were dreading the eight-hour drive, so on a whim I booked us on a turboprop, a puddle jumper that took us to Medford. My wife dropped us off at the airport early, and as we walked across the tarmac I knew what Dave was thinking, because I was thinking it too.

We squeezed onto that 20-seater and looked out the window at the propeller, and we both started to laugh. We'd spent many hours in the dark, you see, in retrospective theaters in our early 20s, watching films from the forties, the great ones. We were on familiar terms with John Garfield and James Cagney, Paul Muni and Bogie and Bacall. So we knew what images were floating through each other's mind.

We were heading for Lisbon, for the clipper to America, escaping the Nazis and saying goodbye to Casablanca, leaving Claude Raines to round up the usual suspects, and we laughed all the way to Oregon, because that's what friends are for.

(9/15/04)

Moving On

A friend of mine, a few years back, quit his corporate job and decided to write a book about a subject he loved. It was a planned and well-thought-out midlife leap, discussed and budgeted, and he approached it with the discipline of a man who knew the water was deep but wanted to swim anyway.

After a year or so, though, he was running low on money and took a job as a temporary mail carrier, no benefits and no career track, just a way to make some money and, as an added and unexpected bonus, lose some weight.

He gained some insight, too, as you might expect from a writer, and there would be times when we'd walk outside, after meeting for lunch or some other reason, and he'd look at the sky and say, "This would be a bad day to deliver mail" and I would just nod, only sort of understanding.

I have a better appreciation of mail carriers, then, having heard some stories, but then I always have. They bring news, after all, good and bad, along with flyers and report cards and pieces of paper that say "Pay To The Order Of," and sometimes they bring closure, notice of the end of something and the beginning, hopefully, of another.

As happened this past weekend, but let me digress.

One score and three years ago, more or less, I took a temporary job of my own, although I had no way of knowing back then exactly what and for how long. My first 26 years, looking back, seemed lacking a little in direction. I had made decisions, of course, and taken risks and dreamed my dreams, but life still seemed awfully open-ended with limitless choices, and I was a boat in search of a rudder and one morning in 1984 I got one.

You can choose, you see, when the alarm rings at 6.

You can shower and dress and head for work, or roll over and whisper into the phone words about a cough and low-grade fever and take the day off, or even say rude words to your boss and burn your bridges. You have options, lots of them, but as it turns out when the baby wakes up and starts to cry, your choices go out the window. You get up and feed her, or change her or comfort her, and that's just what you do.

I liked that, I found out, the discipline of duty. My days were suddenly easier, more defined and structured, less open-ended. I was a parent, and that was not just who I was but how and why, in some way, and I liked it so much that five years later I got a promotion.

By then, though, when my son was born, I knew the routine. I knew about teething and colic and pediatricians. I knew how to heat formula and pin a diaper without drawing blood, or to change it without throwing up.

I learned about parent-teacher conferences and soccer games and orchestra concerts, about rolling eyes and phone bills and car insurance, and four years ago I learned about letting go.

If you've been reading this column for the past few years (and really, haven't I apologized enough?), you might remember some whining and wailing in print on my part when my daughter graduated from high school. I took it hard; it felt like I was done, somehow, and I wasn't ready.

And then she decided to go to college in Texas, and I got thrown again. My daughter just shook her head and tried to ignore my silliness. "It's only four years," she'd say, "and then I'll come back home" but it felt final to me, and I lost it for a while.

Now I shake my own head at my own silliness. The past four years have moved quickly, almost effortlessly, as we all have grown. She learned, had success and maybe some minor failures, got jobs and passed exams.

She ended her fourth year with 4 credits remaining for her degree, which she finished this summer while putting the pieces together for the rest of her life.

She and Cameron, her significant other, have both landed jobs in Boston, a city they love and one that excites Dad, too, visions of American history and day tours dancing through my head. They've been negotiating long distance, firming up details and a place to live, and then last week, almost as an afterthought, the graduation announcement arrived in the mail and my wife and I read it, proud but calm.

I've graduated, too, passed through trauma and midlife angst, and life is good, even surprising. This is the summer of my content, I realized the other day, and I've come to appreciate choices again, and open-ended futures.

So I just smiled at the piece of paper, announcing what I already knew, and I wandered back to the bedroom and then into the bathroom, where I locked the door. My lower lip had begun to quiver, unexpectedly. You'd think I'd have outgrown emotion of this sort but you'd be wrong, I guess, and you'd be wrong if you thought it was about pride, or relief.

It was about me, but then really it always was, and I thought, "But she said she would come home," and I stayed there a while, knowing it would pass.

(7/18/07)

The Journey

It was a one-sided conversation, to say the least.

He was lying down on the cold concrete, his breathing rapid and shallow. For a long time, he wouldn't meet my eyes, even as I got down close and spoke softly. He obviously had seen better days. "What do you need?" I asked. "What can I get you?' It was as if I weren't even there.

Finally, I hit on the right words. "Do you want something to eat?" His head jerked a bit, and he began to move, slowly, painfulyl, old joints trying to remember, and as he staggered to his feet he finally looked at me.

And barked. A couple of times.

Hey, I was home alone last week. Sometimes you have to make do with the company you have.

There was a time, years ago, when I would have relished the better part of three days by myself, my only companion a dog who didn't make small talk. I would have basked in the peace and quiet, walked around the house in my underwear, had sole control of the remote control, and eaten as many burritos as I wanted. The good life, in other words.

Something happened along the way, though. The kids got older and more independent, my wife got very busy, and demands upon my precious time mostly centered around running out to get more milk and trying to remember not to sleep on my back.

So it was a little lonely, surprisingly so. I missed the ambient sounds, the music and the conversations, even the beeps and whistles of the occasional video game. I missed the sound of the piano, and the sound of big teenager feet clomping about at all hours, searching for snacks.

I missed my son.

The plans started about a month ago. My wife was scheduled to spend a week in July at a conference. She does this a lot, usually in the summer, leaves home and recharges her batteries, and while we always manage, as the years go by a middle-aged man and a teenage boy begin to find personality conflicts, and not in the good way. So I stared ahead at our week alone and wondered how it'd go this year.

It was his sister who came up with the idea. "Send John to Texas," she said, and God love her for that. May she have a speedy recovery.

My daughter lives in North Texas, where she's beginning her senior year in college. She has a house, a boyfriend, a job and summer school, but she also has a brother and an awareness of summer blues, so she threw out the idea and suddenly it was a reality. He was going to Texas, and I was going to learn a lesson in letting go.

My son has never traveled alone. He was born with a neurological condition that makes it difficult, if not impossible, for him to read body language and facial expressions, the sort of thing most of us do naturally. So socializing with strangers can be awkward at best, sort of like telling a color-blind guy that the men's room door is painted blue, not pink, that's how you tell. Chances are good that mistakes will be made, and anxiety is never far from the surface.

Mostly his father's anxiety, as it turned out. When I brought up the subject of a four-hour flight to Dallas alone, he raised an eyebrow, thought for a minute, and then offered his opinion that it was about time. He was right, but that didn't help Dad's digestion.

Add to that the fact that his mom was out of town, taking her organizational skills with her, and for a couple of days I scrambled and sweated. The morning of his flight I was up at 3 a.m., trying to remember what I'd forgotten, while he just got dressed and was the picture of calm.

I persuaded the airlines to let me accompany him to the

gate, more for my benefit than his, so for an hour we sat there, looking out the window, while I tried to think of reassuring things to say and he rolled his eyes. Get a grip, Dad. It's just a plane trip.

Finally the attendant called his row, and he grabbed his backpack, stuck out his hand, and said, "You can go now," and I suddenly knew it was a moment I hadn't seen coming. I held him in my arms when he was one minute old. I took him to swimming and tennis lessons, taught him how to ride a bike, made him pancakes and dropped him off at school, and now it was time to go. For both of us.

I stood on the sidelines, too scared to say anything that might embarrass him, and watched as he moved through the line, showed his boarding pass, and walked onto the plane. And really he never looked back, not even once.

(7/19/06)

Home Alone

A couple of weeks ago, my wife and son left me alone for a few days. Not in the "please leave me alone" way, but in the packed bags, full tank, don't-forget-to-feed-the-dog way.

There were times in my life when that was sort of a thrill, solitude and space. A friend of mine once summed up the situation pretty well, having the women and children in our lives out of the house for an extended period of time, leaving us to our own devices.

"It's Pop-Tart time," he said, and he was right.

It's possible that my friend and I are exceptions to the rule (that's come up before, actually), but I suspect there's something in the chromosomes and culture going on here. Something about a taste of anarchy, about freedom from female supervision, about true nature and caged beasts. I could be wrong.

But I ate a couple of frozen pizzas that week, something I never do, and I stayed up real late watching spy movies. Ice cream was also involved, as were unmade beds and some really loud music.

The problem with pretending that you're a 15-year-old and your parents are gone for the weekend can be found in the Second Law of Thermodynamics, which notes that entropy always increases. "Entropy," in this particular case, refers to the irreversible aging of the human gastrointestinal system. I should have a T-shirt made:

"My family went on vacation, and all I got was this stupid heartburn."

Aside from a poor diet, though, and an odd choice of movies (they combined one night to produce a very strange dream, which I decided to call "The Bourne Appendectomy"), I discovered that I've apparently grown out of solitude. There was a time when I craved it, when I dreamed of long, solitary weekends with good books, silence, and no small people asking me to make macaroni and cheese or find a stray Lego, but I'm apparently past that now.

It was lonely. I wandered the aisles of the grocery store, never once going to the produce section, got way too excited over a sale on paper towels, cornered a neighbor I saw and blabbed to him for a good 10 minutes, and whined to my favorite check-out person, Gayle.

"Look at me," I said. "I'm buying frozen pizza and diet soda. What kind of life is this?"

She was sympathetic. "Try Subway," she said, but then she had customers waiting.

My ideas about being industrious went out the window. The bedroom didn't get painted, the bedding didn't get washed, the garage didn't get cleaned and the floor didn't get scrubbed. I listened to talk radio, ran the dishwasher twice by mistake, watched a few Mariners games, and once, when Kenny Loggins' "Footloose" came on my iPod, I tried to do that dance Kevin Bacon did in the movie and I think I broke something.

I couldn't sleep. There was something about having a bed to myself that gave me too many options; I stacked and restacked pillows, I tossed, I turned, I swung my arms around, knowing I wouldn't hit anything human, and still I ended up the next morning sort of sideways, with a sore neck and the dog licking my feet, inquiring about breakfast. The bed looked like someone had searched it for weapons.

I freely admit my domestication, but then I've known that for years. The dirty clothes go in the hamper, milk is to be consumed in a glass and not straight from the carton, the vacuum cleaner and toothpaste cap both have functions, and the toilet seat is to be left down, period. I get that.

I just didn't realize how accustomed I'd become to the company of others, to need and be needed, to share dumb experiences and instant replays of walk-off home runs. For five short days in early August, I became a theoretical human being, a philosophy lesson, an empirical question. If a man is alone in the house, and he stubs his toe, does he make a sound?

Well, yes. He does. He actually makes lots of noises when he's alone, but I don't really want to talk about noises.

The point is, the toe will hurt a lot longer without someone else around to feel sorry for you, even if they might point out that the dining room table has been in that exact same spot for years now and nobody else seems to be stubbing their toes. It's the sympathy that counts.

My wife and son came back late one night, sunburned and covered with mosquito bites, full of stories about the beach and the people, glad to see me and pretending not to notice the pizza boxes.

The next day, John mentioned that he'd missed my super-special macaroni and cheese. I sighed, said "I guess I could make you some," tried to look put out, and failed, of course.

(8/22/07)

Autumn

"My sorrow, when she's here with me, thinks these dark days of autumn rain are beautiful as days can be; she loves the bare, the withered tree; she walks the sodden pasture lane."

--Robert Frost

"I cannot endure to waste anything as precious as autumn sunshine by staying in the house. So I spend almost all the daylight hours in the open air."

--Nathaniel Hawthorne

"Give autumn an inch, and it'll park a day in it so damn beautiful that your teeth will hurt. And then it will rain."

--*When Autumn Leaves*, page 160

When Autumn Leaves

I have a calendar, ten fingers, ten toes, and Internet access, and still I get blindsided once a year, this not being an exception, by the tilt of the planet and the inevitability of October.

I've seen other autumns, you know. In southern California, where I lived as a kid, it was same old, same old, one more nice day. In central Arizona, the fourth season was a reprieve, a stay of execution, time off for good behavior. You survive August in Phoenix just knowing that come October, there will be the World Series and if you don't like baseball at least you can finally walk outside again.

It's different up here, as I learned, a place where leaves actually turn and birds actually fly south. In this neck of the woods, fall is a cautionary tale, a warning shot across the bow, an oil light that blinks for a moment, an old man on a park bench who tells wonderful stories and then says, "You'd best be heading home now, little fella. It's gonna be dark soon."

Fall is my favorite, all crimson and caramel apples. It makes me want to take long walks, go to Friday night high school football games, and put a stock pot on the stove. It's the season that draws out my inner cook, and I want things that do a slow simmer, soup, chili, roasts.

Fall is a riddle wrapped in a mystery inside insulation you always meant to add to the exposed pipes but never got around to doing. It laughs at our expectations and acknowledges our dreams and fears, and sometimes it gets a little playful. Give autumn an inch, and it'll park a day in it so damn beautiful that your teeth will hurt. And then it will rain.

Fall is for going back, for celebrating that one Sunday when you think maybe Daylight Savings Time is not such a bad idea after all, a day when if you're late for church then you have no excuses, none, and you hope maybe the pastor skips the lectionary and instead delivers a homily on Creation, on orange leaves and the goodness of God and gutters that need cleaning, and now.

I've never argued with autumn, or found it practical to do so. Fall is not a debate topic; it simply is what it is, and that would be a signpost that has the word "January" on it, with a big arrow pointing north. They sell firewood in fall, along with Halloween costumes and cinnamon, and on the way home maybe we stop to talk to our neighbors, knowing from experience that barring an unexpected ambulance or a sudden snowstorm, we might not see them again until March. This is autumn's message. Clear the air. Make amends, say goodbyes, repent, apologize, mow the lawn one last time and turn the bolt, winter is coming and you can't stop it, you can't.

This is the liturgy of the last days, sweaters that don't smell that good coming out of the closet and "trick or treat," an odd expression that pretty much sums up the season. We will get both, thank you very much. It's closing time, but take a deep breath before you go. We'll catch you on the flip side.

It's the season to remember the story of the ant and the grasshopper. I admit to having my grasshopper moments, when I'd rather kick leaves than rake them, but autumn serves as a to-do list and some of that needs to be done. The hose will not disconnect itself, no matter how persuasive I am.

Still, it can't be all about responsibility. There are autumn moments to be savored, stored away for future reference when December gets ugly. I never do all I think I will, plan on doing, and some of that is just being realistic. Sure, I dream about wandering into the backyard, picking up a football and tossing it through a tire, just once, one last time, but I know the result would be a wobbly spiral and quite possibly arthroscopic surgery, so I'll skip that, I think.

And I'll probably pass on carving a pumpkin, too, which

is never as fun as it sounds, anyway.

But I'll get out more, breathe crisp air, look at the trees, walk the dog, put the soup on and remember all the other autumns, and remember why. It's nature's way of reminding us that there are stages, that we're not here all that long, and that prioritizing is not so hard, not when it's autumn and we know what's coming.

(10/12/05)

Greece To Me

My birthday is and was July 26, which I noted at the time but you can never mention this sort of thing too much if you ask me. It's a day I share with Voula, who lives in Greece and wrote me a very nice email the other day. I have no idea how she found me, but I like the idea that I have a Greek reader.

My wife studied Greek, by the way, although I think she's forgotten most of it. Sort of like me and geometry. Which, I believe, was invented by the Greeks, so there you go. I see a pattern.

My wife also might find it interesting that I get emails from Greek women, so we just won't tell her.

This summer, it was a quiet Chuck-Voula Day, and that was fine with me. I think my wife was a little anxious about it, because she was going to be out of town and also because she just gets a little anxious about me from time to time. So I tried to put her mind at ease.

"I'll be fine, honey. I have work to do, after all, and John will probably sleep late, and Scott will drop by and maybe we'll watch some of the Democratic Convention or see a movie, and maybe if by that time I have a DVD burner I'll start transferring our videotapes onto DVD with my new DVD burner, which I really think would be useful and fun if I had a DVD burner, which I would never buy for myself."

That seemed to make her relax a bit.

So. Now I have this George Foreman Grill.

This is because my wife is smarter and more practical than I am. I mean, after I burn a bunch of DVDs of the endless hours of videotape of my baby daughter sleeping, what would I do with it?

My George Foreman Grill, on the other hand, I use all the time.

See, my wife understands this. A few years ago, she bought me an iced tea maker. You might wonder why you'd need a machine to make iced tea, but this was a clever idea that I wish I'd thought of first. Someone figured out the right combination of water and ice, so that the tea brews and melts the ice just enough that you have iced tea in 10 minutes, cold and everything.

Since I drink a lot of iced tea, I use this machine all the time. And one day, waiting for my tea, I noticed that we also had a bread machine that nobody seemed to be using, so I made some bread, and then, after a while, I decided that it might be fun to toss the machine and make bread the old-fashioned way, and soon I was devouring cookbooks and roasting chickens and making soup and Hunan-style pork roast with wild rice and grapes and steamed vegetables. I became a cooking fool.

So my wife probably figured I'd start using this grill and maybe, I dunno, begin washing windows or picking my underwear off the floor. She's pretty clever.

Fiendishly clever.

I use my George Foreman Grill mostly for burgers, although I've done chicken breasts and salmon, along with shrimp and assorted veggies. I've also experimented a bit. The other night I attempted to use it to cook a couple of seasoned chicken leg quarters, which is sort of like trying to get a sumo wrestler into a tanning booth. Coverage is going to be questionable.

And once in a while, when I'm in a mood, I'll cook a whole pound of bacon, Elvis style. Man, that George Foreman Grill can cook some mean bacon. Crisp if you like, or chewy if you're brave, but I can cook a slab o' bacon in 20 minutes and I do, I really do. I don't eat it all at once, you understand. I just cook it that way.

Dear George Foreman:

My name is Chuck. My wife gave me one of your grills for my birthday, which is also Voula's birthday, who lives in Greece. Do you sell your grills in Greece? You might want to think about it.

I enjoy your product, but I have a suggestion.

This one would have a bigger lid, big enough to cover chicken quarters. And it would have room for a whole pound of bacon, if not two. And it would have something, I don't know, a needle or something, that would test your cholesterol level constantly. And it would make iced tea, and maybe bread.

And (this is VERY IMPORTANT), it would, at the same time, burn DVDs. I can't emphasize this aspect too much.

You can have this idea for free, by the way. Just say, "Idea From Chuck," something like that.

Did you ever notice that "Greece" sounds almost exactly like "grease?" There's a marketing tool there, I bet. You can have that for free, too.

I am eating a piece of George Foreman Grill-cooked bacon right now, as a matter of fact. Mmm, mmm. Very tasty. Although suddenly my chest is hurti

(9/29/04)

A Cool Hand

I have anecdote envy sometimes, not quite split evenly between professional and personal. There are writers I go to in certain situations, for example, when someone famous passes away, knowing they'll have interesting thoughts and maybe some personal experiences with the departed to share and fill out the picture for us a little. It'd be nice to have a fuller life, I mean; I can only milk my dog and lawn for so much material.

At the same time, I've always had little fantasies of chance meetings with famous people I'd admire -- there I am, headphones plugged in and my nose in a book, ready to endure a boring flight somewhere, and suddenly Bruce Willis plops down in the seat next to me (I have no particular feelings for Mr. Willis one way or the other; he's a neutral fantasy, for publication purposes only). We have a four-hour conversation and at the end I've got a new friend. Hey, it could happen.

So in the midst of all this craziness, politics and finance, suspended campaigns and equity-swap-something crises that threaten our way of life, late-night meetings of leaders and press conferences and political ads and fact checkers and oh by the way your bank went belly up last night, try not to panic, the death of a movie star seemed at first like Just More Bad News and then time for reminiscing, and I had nothing. Nada.

I can tell you lots of stories about me and Paul Newman, of course, but only of the one-way variety.

For those of us who love movies, what we saw and when we saw it sometimes makes more of a difference that any earthshaking events we've lived through. We might measure our worldview by generational standards -- I watched a war as a kid, you were 10 years older and eying draft registration, it makes a difference – but who we are and what we think might be influenced even more by our ages when we first saw "Cool Hand Luke." In this case, anyway.

That film, by the way, is my earliest recollection of Paul Newman, and I saw it from the backseat of the family car, surrounded by pillows and popcorn; drive-ins, a rarity these days, dead and dying, were the only choice for parents with three young kids who liked movies, so I saw a lot of films in the 1960s from the station wagon, and I remember that one well.

It was a few years later, though, that Mr. Newman took up permanent residence. Another drive-in, another backseat, but this time it was "Butch Cassidy and the Sundance Kid." It had a strong and specific appeal: I didn't come out of it wanting to be an outlaw or a cowboy, although I won't argue the appeal. I wanted to be an actor, and in particular I wanted to play Butch, funny, handsome, charming, and having vision while the rest of the world wore bifocals. I spent a lot of years trying.

You've read the articles by now, if you're interested, so I can't tell you anything you don't already know. The films, the awards, the charities, the racing, the long and lovely marriage. He seemed like a nice man, a decent man, an ordinary one who did extraordinary things, and he died last week at 83 in his home, surrounded by family, having managed to live his life without ever once encountering me. And so, as I say, I've got nothing.

But I could have, I realized the other day. I was THIS close.

In 1979, a friend and I managed to wrangle passes onto the Warner Brothers lot in Burbank. We wandered around, not having any luck at being accidentally discovered as the next Newman and Redford (for good reason), spent a few minutes watching busy people film an episode of "The Dukes of Hazzard," and then as we were leaving we saw the parking space.

It was in front of the looping building, where actors re-record dialogue that was muffled or otherwise needed fixing. There were two spaces in front with names prominently painted on them. One said "Dustin Hoffman" and in it was parked an unremarkable Datsun 240Z.

And the other was "Mr. Paul Newman," and it had a Porsche. A Porsche that had a license plate decal that said, "I'd Rather Be Racing."

Oh, you betcha that was his car.

We waited for a few minutes, trying to tweak chance, but Butch had better things to do than brighten up our days.

That's my anecdote, then, the encounter that almost was, or might have been. I salute you, anyway, Mr. Newman, for your life and the hours of pleasure I got watching you work, which I was reminded of from the many news stories I saw over the past weekend.

Including a clip from "The Verdict," one of my favorites, in which you can see, in Newman's final courtroom scene, an extra, playing an audience member in the background, looking very serious, listening intently.

Pause it. Take a good look. Don't let the hair fool you; it's a very young, and very unknown, actor by the name of Bruce Willis.

I'll bet he has some anecdotes.

But I touched the car. That's gotta count for something.

(10/1/08)

Zeno Hits the Road

Of all the technical things I consider myself adept at, including replacing an air filter and boiling water, among their number (which would be about five, anyway) you won't find the ability to draw worth a whit.

I'm pretty sure I couldn't draw an actual whit, either.

It's not that all I'm capable of are stick figures. I have some sense of light and shadow, and if I'm in the mood I can be patient and take my time. It's just that I seem to lack a sense of perspective. Noses are too big for faces, the vanishing point always vanishes in the wrong place, and you really don't want to see me attempt trees. It's ugly.

It occurred to me recently that maybe my deficiency has to do with the fact that a fair amount of my childhood was spent sort of monocular. It wasn't until I was 13 that we discovered my left eye was bad, something like 20/100 while my right was 20/20. So maybe I was always seeing a skewed world.

I wore corrective lenses after that, at first the right one essentially clear, and in fact I was in my 20s before I couldn't get away with leaving the glasses at home while I was working or trying to impress some female-type person. Now I'm just as blind as a bat. Take my glasses away and I'm pretty helpless. I'm probably legally not even allowed to walk without them.

I've been thinking a lot about perspective lately.

As I told a friend the other day, working at home for 16 years can stunt one's growth. There are lots of everyday reference points that tend to go missing. In some ways, it's back to monocular. I seem to have misplaced a little depth.

I've been thinking about this, and a lot of what I think has to do with how, maybe, to regain a little dimension, a little height, depth and width (insert joke here).

So my son and I took a trip.

We used to travel a lot, the two of us. One of my best memories is of taking him to Disneyland when he was 8. It was Boyland, too, just us, riding the rides as many times as we wanted, crashing in our hotel and then doing the same thing the next day. And there were other trips, mostly to Arizona to visit the grandparents. We got used to being travel partners.

It's been a while, though, so after some consultation we headed out Saturday morning to Eugene to meet up with my brother and his son. The boys are the same age, and we figured it might be fun, and it was.

Driving through southern Washington at dawn is a good way to shake some staleness and cobwebs, as it turns out, along with some father-son conversation and an ice chest of Dr. Pepper.

As I've written before, one of my favorite metaphors comes from Zeno's Paradox. Zeno, that wacky Ancient Greek, postulated that motion was an illusion. That is, to travel from Point A to Point B, you first have to go to Point A-1/2. To walk a hundred yards, you first have to walk 50 yards, and before that 25, and before that 12-1/2, and before that 6-1/4, and before that fractions are hurting my head now so I'll stop. Since you always have to go halfway first, and since any distance can be divided in half, you never go anywhere.

My solution to this, as I've also written before, is that in order to get somewhere else, you only need to know where you started.

We had a good time, the four of us, wandering the University of Oregon campus, swimming in the hotel indoor pool, going to a street fair, throwing our clothes all over the hotel room, eating pizza, etc. But it was on the trip back, when John decided sleeping for 300 miles was the better part of valor, that I got some perspective back, and none too soon.

It suddenly struck me that it's been 22 years this week since my wife and I made that same northward I-5 trek, no jobs in store, 500 bucks in our pockets and a trailer filled with all our stuff, looking for our future.

And it's been four years, also this week, since I began this column.

I'm different than I was four years ago, and certainly far different than I was in 1983. So much of it has been a blank page, waiting to be filled.

So, as I say, you know you're moving as long as you remember that once you were somewhere else. And sometimes it just takes getting away, out of the house, to remind us that we're always heading somewhere, and we always have to go halfway first, and part of the joy of the journey is not having a clue as to where we're going to end up, just knowing it will be some place different.

(10/05/05)

Asking Good Questions

The Devil slid into Snohomish County last week, causing trouble and carrying an invoice.

It didn't cross our minds last July that there would be consequences. We were too busy, maybe, firing up the grill or slipping into the Sound for a couple of hours in the early evening to reckon the cost, but here it is. There's a price to be paid for summer, the Devil will always get his due, and the bottom line on the bill has one word: October.

I still love it, this month, even with our recent weather. October is the time for tying up loose ends, cleaning gutters and disconnecting hoses, addressing nagging problems that seemed minor in the sunshine but take on new urgency once the rain starts. It's a welcome party for winter, a nice show of support before we all hunker down for the duration. See you in June.

Baseball winds down, basketball warms up, and football shakes out, winners and losers starting to get clearer. School has developed a rhythm, churches pick up the stragglers, and there are lots and lots of pumpkins. I like October just fine.

It's also a time for nostalgia. I find myself remembering other Octobers, particularly the one 24 years ago, when my wife and I staggered into Seattle, hauling a trailer and wondering what we could have been thinking, so far from all we knew as home. It was a sunny fall in 1983, though, and we fell in love with the Northwest, and kind people were discreet and never mentioned November.

There were other Octobers, though, and other times I don't remember but should, and so I've spent a fair amount of time this fall watching "The War."

I haven't seen the whole thing yet; thanks to the magic of DVRs and DVD burners, I've got Ken Burns' latest documentary on disk, allowing me to watch when I can, but I've seen enough to know this is another good one.

Over as six-year period, Burns managed to pull off a feat bordering on divination. We've seen plenty of documentaries, plenty of footage and plenty of commentary on World War II, but missing have been the millions of men who left their families and their homes and went to war, and then came home.

And wouldn't talk. It's become so familiar that it's a cliché, but it's also truth for frustrated historians and family members. Unlike generations of warriors to come, the men who returned after that war mostly stayed silent. They went back to work, raised families and picked up their lives, but what they'd done and what they'd seen was left, mostly, unsaid.

They're leaving us, though, now at a rate of 1100 a day, and Mr. Burns deserves his credit for coaxing some fascinating portraits out of ordinary people who lived in extraordinary times.

Some of it isn't for the squeamish. No matter how just and noble and necessary the cause, and this was all three, war is the underbelly of civilization, ugly and cruel and base. It was, I imagine, a daily struggle to hold onto humanity in the face of terror and horror. No wonder they're reluctant to talk.

So in addition to the voices on "The War," it was surprising to see some veterans speak up last week. These were the men of Fort Hunt, a top-secret project to interrogate Nazi prisoners of war, silent for 60 years until now.

It may have been simply that it was time. Or it may have been this particular time, but out of two dozen veterans more than a few had words to say about what they did, and what's being done today in their names.

They bugged cells, read mail, and softened up their prisoners at Fort Hunt, often playing games with them. "We got more information out of a German general with a game of chess or Ping-Pong than they do today, with their torture," said Henry Kolm, 90.

John Gunther Dean, 81, said, ""We did it with a certain amount of respect and justice."

"During the many interrogations, I never laid hands on anyone," said George Frenkel, 87.

Peter Weis, 82, put it more bluntly. "I am deeply honored to be here, but I want to make it clear that my presence here is not in support of the current war."

Do we write them off as out of touch, senile and uncomprehending of the evil we face in this century? Do we minimize Dachau and Bataan as incomparable to 9/11? Do we think they just don't get it? Are they the "phony soldiers" Rush Limbaugh was referring to?

Or do we listen to the men of Fort Hunt, and think about what they saw and what they have to say?

"We don't torture," President Bush says, but a reasonable person would have to say that we do. Water boarding, sleep deprivation, humiliation, forced exposure to cold, threatening with dogs. Rape. Murder. The stories are out there, witnessed and documented.

This may well be the legacy of the Iraq occupation, overshadowing the how and the why of war: The way we conducted ourselves when faced with evil, and how it compares to when we faced it once before.

"We extracted information in a battle of the wits," Mr. Frenkel said. "I'm proud to say I never compromised my humanity."

He should be proud, and us of him. And we should listen, because this war will eventually end, and as sure as October rolls around every year the Devil will get his due, and be in the details.

(10/10/07)

The Man of Steel

I love movie trailers. Creating them is an art form, a specialized skill that can make money for a poor film and enhance a superior one. I rarely get out to the movies these days, but when I do I get there early. Sometimes Coming Attractions are the best part.

I can still remember previews from years ago. The one for "Jaws II," for example, I remember as being striking, considering (in retrospect) what a lousy movie that was. The one for "Bram Stoker's Dracula" gave me chills. "Jurassic Park" made me wonder if that was something I really wanted to see (I did).

The film trailer I remember the most, though, was in 1978. The film I came to see is lost in my memory now, but the music started, there was a frenzy of quick cuts, a flash of red and blue, and then the narration, simple, direct, and perfect:

"You will believe a man can fly."

There were echoes of childhood for me. I was a huge Superman fan, waiting every afternoon for the old 1950s television show to come on ("Look! Up in the sky!").

It's now family lore for us, how I wandered around wearing a pair of my mother's old glasses just so I could whip them off at the appropriate moment, bouncing around the house with a red towel around my neck, bunched up under my shirt. What I would have given for a phone booth in the backyard.

It was a good effort, that first "Superman" film in 1978, although it looks a little cheesy now. Still, it had Gene Hackman as Lex Luther, some nice (for the time) effects, and it was carried by a simple casting decision that made the difference. They found the perfect Man of Steel.

Christopher Reeve was a serious student of acting, going to Cornell and then spending some time at Julliard, where he became friends with another student, a sort of crazy, energetic guy by the name of Robin Williams, a

177

friendship that endured. It was Williams who came through in the dark days after Reeve's 1995 accident, providing moral and financial support.

Reeve was 25 when he was cast as Superman, 6'4 and handsome but a little on the skinny side. They played around with prosthetic muscles but he hated that, so he got a trainer and bulked up. Hard work, apparently, was not a challenge.

There would be other challenges, of course.

He spent a fair amount of time trying to "ditch the cape," as he put it. He was an actor first and foremost, and probably had no desire to leave a legacy of blue tights and a big "S" on his chest. And, as it turned out, he wouldn't.

If there is a more ironic true story that Christopher Reeve in recent years, I don't know it. The man who became famous playing an invulnerable super hero suffered the cruelest blow to an active lifestyle, a devastating spinal cord injury that left him motionless and dependent on others for his very breath. An accident, a tumble from a horse that could have resulted in only bruised skin and ego, could have, cost him his freedom.

And allowed him to ditch the cape, finally, and show us that heroes come in the off-screen variety, too.

It's enough just to manage, we think, it's brave just to keep on living in the face of an injury like this, but Christopher Reeve didn't want to just keep on living. He wanted to walk, and he wanted others to.

Yes, he had resources. He had money and fame. He was in a better position than most. But he never gave up, never lost the hope, and if he did he told us about that, too, and then moved on.

Spinal cord injury sufferers owe him a huge debt, for he forced the issue, changed the paradigm, re-wrote the rules. It's not a stretch for me to believe that one day many people will walk once again solely because

Christopher Reeve couldn't, and refused to accept that.

I wrote another column this week, a dumb thing, trying to lighten things up in a nasty political season, and then I logged on and saw the news, and I remembered sitting in a dark theater and believing, at least for a couple of hours, that a man could fly.

And I remembered the other story, the man in the wheelchair and on the respirator, the humor he displayed, the courage, the determination. He believed he would walk again one day, and if ultimately his body failed him, his spirit never did.

His screen legacy is brief, with a few bright moments and one iconic role, but there's more to a life than pretend. More to his life.

Goodbye, Mr. Reeve. Thanks for your activism, for your courage and your commitment. Thanks for making a difference, for opening our eyes, for enlightening us, and for reminding us that even broken bodies have souls, and some special ones just soar.

(10/13/04)

Playing Tricks

Maybe it was this dumb shoulder. Or maybe it was the autumn weather, or the changing leaves, or Halloween being just around the corner. Or maybe it was just time.

I have no clue about how my brain works, other than to note that it stops at the worst possible times. Still, like everyone else, I suppose, I have moments when a stray thought snags a memory or three, and it comes out of the blue.

My shoulder issues, by the way, directly relate to the above-mentioned brain function. It was bad enough that I thought I could play a little softball – me, a near-sighted, overweight middle-aged man whose recreation of choice usually involves the supine position.

But no. A fly ball soared over my head, as fly balls tend to do, and instead of watching it I decided to run backwards, a skill, like speaking Spanish or solving a geometry proof, I apparently have lost. At least I ended up supine.

I tore my rotator cuff, that collection of muscles and ligaments that keeps the shoulder joint doing what shoulders are supposed to do. Or at least that's the working diagnosis; by the time you read this, I'll have had an MRI and we'll know more.

What I do know at this time is that I need my shoulder, and preferably both of them. It can come in handy when putting on deodorant, for example.

So I was sitting on the back deck, feeling sorry for myself, rubbing my shoulder, looking at the leaves, feeling the crisp fall air, thinking about Halloween coming up, and suddenly there he was.

My father was born in Springfield, Missouri on December 7, five years before that date became infamous. His childhood was mostly a mystery to him, cloudy and vague. His parents were divorced, and he spent some time being shuttled between family and foster care. He grew up fast.

By the time he was a teenager, though, life had settled somewhat and he fit right into the Fifties. I have a picture of him from back then, blue jeans and white T-shirt, a goofy grin on his face and a cigarette dangling from his lips. Always a cigarette.

He married his high school sweetheart and was a father by the time he was 19. He got a job as an apprentice orthotist, someone who makes braces (not the kind that go on your teeth). He was good at it and got better, being a natural craftsman and having a preternatural ability to immediately see how things worked and fit.

I watched him work with patients from time to time, and saw something different. The quick-tempered, perfectionist, often inpatient man I knew was gentle and soothing with people who were suffering. He joked and worked quickly, and everyone seemed to like my dad. As I said, he knew was he was doing.

He quit smoking, after half a century, in the beginning of 2003 at the age of 66. He was feeling bad, tired and out of sorts, and he thought it would help. It didn't, as it turned out; cancer was already spreading from his lungs through his lymphatic system to his liver.

The prognosis wasn't great, but Dad never gave up hope as far as I knew. He went through chemotherapy and kept making plans, for trips or going back to work or his 50th wedding anniversary in 2005. And eventually, at the end of therapy, his cancer was gone.

It was a Wednesday, October 29. I was heading out the door when I got a call from my mother.

"You have to be very strong now," she said.

Dad had been falling, and a CT scan showed over fifty tumors in his brain. Game almost over. I called the airline.

There were some kids in costumes on my flight that Friday night, Halloween, and the stewardess handed out candy. It was a strange sensation, flying over small towns and cities, knowing what was happening in the streets below, knowing I was heading home to say goodbye to my father. Flying southeast to Arizona. Flying into darkness, as it happened.

So maybe it was just Halloween, the time of year bringing back a memory. That makes sense.

I think, though, that maybe it was the shoulder after all. My father knew his way around muscles and joints, and he would have had a thing or two to say about my situation, once he got through laughing at the image of me taking a tumble. And if he'd been around, I imagine he'd have taken a look himself, taken the joint through a range of motion, gently manipulating and testing, wondering if he could help.

Things change in three years. Loss is slipped between pages to rest in the past, and we move on. This is just life; it happens to all of us.

There was something about the moment, though. Almost a chill, and not from the breeze. It's hard to describe, and harder to explain, but I guess I would say that if you think from to time I don't feel a strong, familiar hand on my shoulder, you don't know me very well, and you certainly didn't know my father.

(10/25/06)

Fifty-Fifty

I'm a fan of The Fifties, and have been for a long time. I mentioned this in an e-mail birthday wish to my buddy, Clarence in Kentucky, who turned 65 on October 26. I've always accused Clarence of being Fonzie all grown up, a charge he accepts proudly.

Some of it is the music, of course, and some the movies. Some of it has to do with hearing stories from my parents, and some, I'm a little embarrassed to say, came from serious exposure to "Happy Days" in the 1970s.

It's odd how that particular decade is often described as placid, calm, a respite from war and the Depression. It was that, surely, but it also was a time that kicked up its heels and started us down several interesting paths. The Fifties has legs.

The interstate highway system. The birth control pill. Rock 'n' roll, TV dinners (TV, for that matter), Buddy Holly and Jimmy Dean, the Bates Motel and "Stella!" Mass-produced neighborhoods and the genesis of suburbia. The Dodgers and the Yankees. Holiday Inns all over the place, suddenly.

There was Ed Cole, a man lost to anonymity now but who left his fingerprints all over the automotive industry, a driven, compulsive genius of an engineer who never saw a machine he couldn't fix and make better and whose greatest achievement, a V-8, 160-horsepower baby that to car enthusiasts and the rest of us was and is simply called the '55 Chevy.

Or Dick and Maurice, two brothers from New Hampshire who moved to California in the 30s, looking for work. They tried the movie theater business and a hot dog stand, neither all that successful. Moving to San Bernadino, they opened up a drive-in restaurant with all sorts of sandwiches, burgers and barbecue on the menu. They started making good money, but noticed that pretty carhops attracted teenage boys who clogged the parking lot, and also discovered that their top-heavy menu was still producing mostly orders for hamburgers.

So they closed the store for three months, redesigned the kitchen, cut the menu by two-thirds, sent the carhops on their way, figured out that infrared lights kept burgers warm for a long time, switched entirely to paper plates and cups, and suddenly there were long lines and lots of interest in copying their formula.

When they finally, reluctantly, sold their first franchise to an Arizona businessman, they were astonished that he wanted to keep their name above his restaurant. "What the hell for?" asked Dick. "McDonald's means nothing in Phoenix."

The word "superstar" hadn't been coined yet, but the 50s produced its share, in sports, film, television and politics. Few would have much in the way of longevity, such is fame, either from self-destruction (Marilyn Monroe, Joseph McCarthy), a limited public attention span, or just simply attrition. In fact, of all the iconic players in the drama that was the 1950s, I can think of only two who made it into the 21st century with some viability still intact: an odd couple, Marlon Brando and Billy Graham.

And the quiet lady.

In the past week or so, we've been reminded of the story of Rosa Parks, both the moment and the myths. No, it wasn't just that she was having a bad day, tired feet, etc. She was already an activist, a secretary of the local NAACP. If it hadn't been that day, it would have been another. She was, in fact, a movement just waiting to be asked to move.

On Monday of this week, nearly fifty years to the day from that bus ride in Montgomery, Rosa Parks laid in state in the Capitol Rotunda, a place reserved for fallen presidents, the first woman ever to share that honor. And if that strikes some as perhaps political, an effort to drive the news cycle away from Scooter, well, then, it

184

might also be noted that the Secretary of State, fourth in line for the presidency, grew up in the 50s and 60s in the war zone that was Alabama as an African-American girl, and surely had some thoughts on the matter.

It's gender, actually, that interests me most in the passing of Rosa Parks. She was a woman.

She had to be. A black man refusing to surrender his seat in the segregated South risked fates worse than a misdemeanor arrest. A 42-year-old woman was merely an annoyance, or so it was thought.

The most important American social movement of the last century (and it has stiff competition) was given a running start by a seamstress who said no. Quietly, gently, firmly, and in a way that resonates and echoes to today. Ms. Rice is her heir. Oprah too.

But also Hillary Clinton. And my wife, and my daughter.

My sister. My mother.

The system of the 1950s was racist but also patriarchal. And it still is, but less so, and partly if not mostly due to an African-American woman who said no, and yes, and at the same time, and for the same reason. And if her name is linked forever with civil rights, then we need to understand, as Dr. King often mentioned, that "civil" and "rights" apply to all of us.

It took a woman, as it turns out. Who goes to her rest now, 92 years in this life, singular and random and marked by history, and perhaps not all that random, and perhaps free at last.

(11/02/05)

Blind Leading the Blind

I don't care for stereotypes, particularly when it comes to men and women. Oh, sure, it's okay to make a joke occasionally, and there are certainly differences between the sexes, but we're complex creatures, individuals and unique, and broad generalizations do us all an injustice.

So I'll just say that some men -- SOME men -- marry their navigators.

This would be me.

It's not that I can't read a map, although, on the other hand, it might be exactly that. Mostly, though, I lack a spatial sense, I think. I'm pretty good with up and down, and I'm working on left and right, but give me directions and tell me to head east and I've pretty much got a 25% chance of getting where I need to go. So I rely on my wife.

Now, in order to understand what happened last Tuesday, there are several things you need to know.

I live in Western Washington. But you probably figured that out.

My daughter lives in Texas. I may have mentioned that once or twice.

On Tuesday nights, my wife teaches a class at Seattle Pacific University, which apparently is in Seattle. Which is south of my house, according to her. That doesn't matter. What matters is that she wasn't here.

On Tuesday night, my daughter decided to make a trip. She'd been planning this, actually. She lives in Denton, Texas, which is a little north of Dallas and a little south of Oklahoma. From what I hear. Her trip was to her grandparents' house, which is in Gun Barrel City, southeast of Dallas, about 100 miles away. An easy trip. A couple of hours.

Which is, I believe, what the Skipper told Gilligan as they left that tropic port aboard that tiny ship.

The weather in Texas has been rough lately. In fact, on

Tuesday her grandparents reported that they were under a tornado watch, and that it was hailing. They advised my daughter to wait until the next day to drive down. Her parents also advised this.

So she went anyway. Because she's invincible. As we neared the two-hour mark, I finally decided to call her cell phone and see how she was doing.

"Guess where I am," she said.

"Um...in Gun Barrel?"

"In DALLAS."

She seemed a little bemused that she'd hit rush hour traffic at 5 in the afternoon. Me, I was not so amused, but maybe she at least learned a lesson. Anyway, she was close to her exit, where she'd pick up another highway, much less congested.

I should also note that my daughter is a registered Democrat. Kids. What are you gonna do? But she's passionate, and was excited about voting in her first presidential election. So excited, in fact, that apparently she plastered her car with bumper stickers. Not just Kerry-Edwards ones. Sarcastic ones. "Send Bush Back to the Ranch," that sort of thing.

Did I mention that she lives in Texas?

So not only was she making a trip, driving it alone for the first time, in questionable weather, but I figured it was possible she might encounter a few drivers along the way who didn't share her political persuasion and possibly were carrying firearms. I was a little nervous.

And then she hit the fog. And got lost.

So I sat there, wifeless, headset plugged into my phone, desperately pulling up maps on my computer that told me nothing, trying to stay calm and speak softly, looking for all the world like an air traffic controller who forgot to tell his boss that he was, you know, blind.

Meanwhile, my 19-year-old daughter was 2000 miles away, careening down I-175 in the dark, in the fog, lost in the middle of boonieville, surrounded by nothing but

187

ranches and broken pick-ups and cows, probably Republican cows, and my wife was gone and I was attempting to give her directions and not start screaming. I could imagine how scared she must have been, all alone, not knowing where she was, not being able to see, probably trembling and terrified and...

"Are you SINGING?" I asked.

"Relax, Dad."

Somehow, though, we got her to Seven Points, which is close enough to Gun Barrel City that you could spit and hit a redneck (sorry; I'm still a little traumatized), so she pulled into a gas station and asked for directions, not being a man. A few minutes later, and some more not really helpful suggestions from me, she was in her grandparents' driveway, low on fuel and hungry but home. And it only took four hours.

The next morning, while she was still asleep, her grandfather took her car up to Wal-Mart and got the oil changed, put air in the tires, and filled up the tank. He's a good grandfather.

It wasn't until he got home that he noticed the bumper stickers.

"I hope nobody saw me," is all he said, but I think that's probably just wishful thinking.

(12/01/04)

George

"Your grandfather has gone visiting," the hospice nurse told Kathy, the oldest. He was between two worlds, she explained, of neither and in both. This wasn't senility but ambivalence, and it left him lost to those who loved him. Where he was going they couldn't follow, and so they kept him warm, and waited. He was 96 years old and it was time, and still each one thought the same thing.

"Please, God, let him have one more Christmas."

You leave some marks in 96 years, some solidness that doesn't break, and more so, maybe, in a small town. Traditions were taken seriously here, and a life of nearly a century, a man born, reared and retired within its limits, was something to be cherished by a city. Many things had changed over the years, so a constant was held in high esteem and this one more than most. There was no one in town, you see, who could remember a Christmas in Bedford Falls without snow, or without George Bailey.

It was an unremarkable life, at least by spectacular standards. A small town banker made few waves in the middle of the 20th century, and if a hundred or so lives were touched, well, still it seemed insignificant in a world of generals and presidents, movie stars and scientists. He was an average man with no headlines tucked away in a scrapbook, and no street signs bearing his name. He had a wife and five children, again unremarkable, and he lived quietly while the world exploded around him, sustained by mediocrity, and Mary.

They were married nearly 25 years, and her death from breast cancer in 1960 seemed an aberration to all, an unnatural act. George became different then, his walk more purposeful and less ambling, and his smile less frequent and more wistful. He sold the family business and dabbled in real estate, painted landscapes, played with his grandchildren, and slowly went deaf, hearing less and watching more.

But nobody kept Christmas like George Bailey. The old house at 320 Sycamore blazed with lights from Thanksgiving Day on, and even well into his 80s George made the rounds, serving up soup at the shelter, passing out gifts, leading carolers through snowy streets, and always, always in the front pew on Christmas Eve, surrounded by family.

As he was surrounded now, he knew, although mostly he played possum, aware of movement but not opening his eyes. He sensed another visitor coming in, pulling a chair up bedside the bed, and still he remained silent.

Until he heard the voice, loud and clear.

"You've been given a great gift, George," said the little man, smiling.

The snow was deep on the street, and they walked in silence for a while, until George had a thought.

"Say! Did you ever get your wings?"

Clarence tried to look miffed.

"Oh, my goodness, of course I did. I'm an angel First Class now, thanks to you, George. You can't get much higher than that, unless..." He sighed and glanced up, almost reproachfully. "Well, we all have our talents, let's say. I'm not very good with weather, for example. And I couldn't smote a fly, even if I wanted to. But I have my moments."

George looked around and shook his head. "So many changes in Bedford Falls. I hardly recognize it anymore."

"Ah, now," said Clarence, brightening. "That's where you're wrong, my good fellow." He glanced up. "Yes, I'm GETTING to it."

"You see, George," he continued, "one thing hasn't changed in all these years, and that's been you."

They were walking by Martini's now, filled as always with customers, celebrating Christmas Eve. "Sixty-two years ago, George, you were given a chance to see what the world would have been like if you hadn't been born. A great gift, as I told you back then. And you've been paying it back ever since."

George stopped, and looked down at Clarence. "You know, I worry about you, little fella. You sure all this snow hasn't soaked your brain?"

"No, George, there's nothing wrong with me. Look here, you mean to tell me you don't realize the gift you've given this town?"

George Bailey thought for a moment. "Well, I suppose..."

Clarence sighed again. "Hope, George. That was your gift. Every questionable loan you made, every chance you took, every kind word you said, every thing you did spoke of hope. Hope like a brand-new morning, hope like a sunrise, hope like a helping hand. Hope like a baby being born, George. Hope like a manger. You could walk into a room and people would see tomorrow. It was a fine gift, George, a fine one."

George ducked his head. "Well... I can tell you a million things --"

"A million wisps, George, a million forgotten moments, all outshone by an aura of goodness. You've made us all proud, George. It was a wonderful life."

"And," he added, "You're going to make a wonderful angel."

George stopped. "Well, now, that's nice, Clarence, but it's late. I've got to be heading home."

"Oh, George," Clarence said, smiling. "You ARE heading home, my friend."

"And I know someone who's waiting for you."

The snow had turned to rain, Kathy noticed, as the minister struggled to abstract nearly a hundred years of life into a graveside service. "No one kept Christmas like George Bailey," he said, invoking Dickens, an odd analogy. Grandpa had been an interesting man, but he'd never been Scrooge, or could be. There was no redemptive moment in his life, no struggle with faith or facing of despair that she knew of, but then she'd been

191

born in 1960 and might have missed some moments.

She watched her mother, now 70 but looking and acting 20 years younger, as she always had, kneel by the casket at the end of the service and do the strangest thing. She scattered rose petals over the lid lightly. "Keep these in your pocket for me, Daddy," she said.

And as they walked back to the car, right on time the bells of First Presbyterian Church of Bedford Falls began to ring, marking the passing of a favorite son, and suddenly Kathy had a thought.

"Do you remember, Mama, what Grandpa used to say whenever he heard a bell ring?"

Zuzu smiled. "I do," she said.

(12/19/07)

About The Author

Chuck Sigars has been writing a weekly column for the Beacon Publishing newspapers in western Washington state since 2001, along with the occasional essay for the Seattle Times, a couple of blogs, various online writing, and something that looked suspiciously like a ransom note but really wasn't (long story).

He continues to be an unnatural tool user, a marginal cook, a haircut waiting to happen and, as it turns out, 50 years old. Although he has lost weight.

He anticipates his next book, a collection of new essays, to be published in 2009. But then he says that all the time.

Made in the USA